Every Moment, Everywhere

*Australian faith stories
to fill up your soul*

Naomi Reed

Published by Acorn Press
An imprint of Bible Society Australia
GPO Box 4161
Sydney NSW 2001
Australia
www.acornpress.net.au | www.biblesociety.org.au
Charity licence 19 000 528

© Naomi Reed 2024. All rights reserved.

ISBN: 978-0-647-53378-9 (print); 978-0-647-53379-6 (ebook)

A catalogue record for this work is available from the National Library of Australia

Apart from any fair dealing for the purposes of private study, research, criticism or review, no part of this work may be reproduced by electronic or other means without the permission of the publisher.

Naomi Reed asserts her right under section 193 of the Copyright Act 1968 (Cth) to be identified as the author of this work.

Unless otherwise indicated, Scripture quotations are taken from the Holy Bible, New International Version® Anglicised, NIV® Copyright © 1979, 1984, 2011 by Biblica, Inc.® Used by permission. All rights reserved worldwide. Quotes marked 'GNT' are from the Good News Translation® (Today's English Version, Second Edition) © 1992 American Bible Society. All rights reserved.

Readers are advised that this book contains references to suicide and substance abuse.

Editor: Kristin Argall
Cover design: SAP
Typesetting: John Healy

Contents

1. My story 1
2. The unravelling 12
3. Trusted friends 42
4. Bible truths 68
5. 'I knew it to be true' 87
6. Beautiful exceptions 101
7. New wineskins 132
8. Go, pour out your gift 158
9. At every age 191
10. Faithfulness to the end 212
Epilogue 239
About the author 243

1
My story

My own story began in a small, suburban home in Sydney, with one older brother, lots of pets and too many camping adventures. I had a vivid imagination, which helped during the camping adventures. Back then, though, I kept most of my thoughts to myself. I was a very quiet child, constantly worried that if I said something out loud, then the words would be wrong and I would be mortified. In order to feel better, I became even quieter. I said less, and it didn't help matters. My teachers and classmates wanted to know what was wrong with me.

At 12, I started high school, and I made one friend. She was the kind of person who seemed to be always smiling. Every Friday, she went to the Christian group at lunchtime (ISCF), and she invited me to go with her. I did, mainly because if I didn't go, then I'd be all alone, and that would be awful.

I remember the first Friday. We sat down on plastic seats in the music room. There were songs and a speaker. The speaker, who was not much older than us, got up and said that there was a God, sovereign over the universe, Maker of everything, holy and just and good ... and longing for relationship with his people – with us. He went on to say that it was true that the world wasn't right, and that we weren't right. We weren't good enough. We mucked things up every day, and we said the wrong things, all the time. But God loved his people so much, that he sent his only Son, the Lord Jesus, to live amongst us and to die for us, to rise again, and to make us right with him, the God of the universe.

I sat there and stared. I felt the truth of it in every part of me. The bell went, and everyone else packed up their lunches and walked to class. I didn't move. I prayed. I said sorry to God, and thank you, and please. I longed to trust in Jesus. My prayer was short and simple, a 12-year-old response. But it genuinely changed everything from that moment on: my view of myself and the world, why I was here, and for what purpose – a tiny part of God's grand story.

Back then, I didn't know anyone else nearby who went to church. My family weren't churchgoers, and my friend lived on the other side of Sydney. But I had a small paperback New Testament, and I read it by myself whenever I could, tucked up in my bed, starting with the Gospel of Matthew. Immediately, I was drawn to Jesus, and his words seemed to ring in my ears. I felt his extraordinary welcome, his healing touch, his upside-down grace and mercy to those who were broken and his challenge to the crowds – and of course, to me. Every word jumped out of the pages, and I underlined them all in different-coloured pens.

I remember the moment I arrived at John 15:12–13. Jesus was speaking to the crowds, and he said, 'My command is this: love each other as I have loved you. Greater love has no one than this: to lay down one's life for one's friends.'

It was absolutely compelling to me, at 12 years old. What does it mean for a 12-year-old to lay down her life for her friends, in response to the consuming love of God? What does it mean for a lifetime?

As I write this, it's been nearly 44 years since that Friday lunchtime in 1980. The question has changed a bit over the years, but essentially it has remained the same. How do I continue to respond to the astounding, costly love of God – for the world, and for me? How do I genuinely love God, and others, for a lifetime?

In late high school, I met Darren and we fell in love. He was kind and funny, and he drove an old brown 1970 Ford Fairmont. After school, we trained together as physiotherapists and then married on a beautiful spring day in 1990. We worked together in Sydney hospitals and enjoyed our local church. Three years later we moved to Nepal, where we worked for six years with a Christian medical mission, the International Nepal Fellowship (INF). Back then, Nepal was a Hindu kingdom, and one of the poorest countries in the world. There were only two Nepali physiotherapists for a population of 20 million people, and one of them was in the UK. The local Nepali church was small and persecuted, and many believers were in prison.

Darren began work as a physio at a regional hospital in Pokhara, alongside wonderful Nepali staff and a few expats, while I worked as a physio at the INF leprosy hospital, also alongside wonderful Nepali staff. Later on, we helped to train local Nepali physios, on a ridge in Dhulikhel, northeast of Kathmandu.

It's hard to describe the privilege of those years. We made the most wonderful friends in the local church and community. They invited us into their lives, and into their Himalayan homes. They taught us to pray, and they embodied God's grace and generosity to us, over and over again. We were challenged, stretched and inspired every single day. We were humbled and encouraged by God's work around us, and most of the time we felt very small. We would do it all over again, if we could!

§

During our third monsoon in Nepal, I gave birth to our first son – a story in itself. We then spent an extended period of time in Australia before returning to Nepal with three sons aged, by then, two, four and eight. If you've ever had three sons, you can imagine the tumbling-around energy and fun during the long plane flight, the settling into a new home (surrounded by goats and buffalo), and our day-to-day life in a foreign country (for another three years) that included driving around on a motorbike that fitted all five of us.

There was another complicating factor in those later years. By 2003, Nepal was in the middle of a civil war. Twelve thousand people had died as a result of a Maoist insurgency. There were regular roadblocks, weekly strikes and occasional bombs. Our house in Dhulikhel was situated halfway up a forested hill, not far from the army camp, so we regularly heard gunfire and wondered if it was real or practice. If it was practice, we could relax. The gunfire would be uniform and predictable. If it was real, we should be under our beds. We quickly learned the difference. There were also shoot-on-sight curfews in place after dark, so we stayed inside in the evenings.

At some point in June 2005, at the beginning of our seventh monsoon, I began to write, mainly to help me think and pray. By then, Darren was very involved in the physio training program at the Dhulikhel Medical Institute. He was doing wonderful work. I was mostly at home, enjoying a slower pace but also feeling hemmed in. I couldn't go out in the mornings because I was homeschooling our three boys. I couldn't go out in the afternoons because of the monsoonal rain. I couldn't go out in the evenings because of the shoot-on-sight curfew. It was hard! On some evenings, I sat quietly at my

1. My Story

desk until midnight, writing, while the rain poured down around me and two candles flickered on either side of the laptop. We had regular power cuts every second evening, which necessitated the candles, and I typed until the battery died.

I thought and prayed, and I wrote about God's purposes through the seasons, especially the hard ones on a Himalayan ridge during civil war and rain and grief and power cuts. I immersed myself in Ecclesiastes and in the Psalms, absorbing God's truth – longing to understand his nature, his ways, his compassion and his patience, in everything. 'There is a time for everything, and a season for every activity under the heavens' (Eccl 3:1). A year later, the writing turned into a book, and we called it *My Seventh Monsoon*. It was published and read quite widely, which was a surprise to both of us. Over the next 15 years, the writing turned into 10 more published books, for adults and children.

As a child and as a young person, I hadn't intended to become a writer. I certainly wasn't drawn to English at school or university. In studying physio, I was immersed in a science-based course. Afterwards, I became reasonably skilled in physical rehabilitation and making prosthetic limbs. But somehow, when the power went off in Dhulikhel and the candles flickered beside me, the writing poured out of me, and I learned much-needed lessons of God's grace to us in Christ. He draws us to himself, even in hardship.

Eight months after that monsoon, in April 2006, we lived through a nationwide revolution in Nepal. Two million people crammed onto the streets of Kathmandu, protesting and demanding that King Gyanendra hand back power to the people. Earlier that month, as a family, we'd been trekking in the Everest region. It was wonderful, but afterwards, we flew straight into Kathmandu – and the revolution. Facing daytime curfews and soldiers on every corner, as well as ongoing nighttime curfews, we decided to hole up in a small hotel room in Kathmandu, ducking out occasionally to buy eggs, bananas and *mithais* (sweets). At the end of April, King Gyanendra gave in, and Nepal became a democratic republic. The 10-year civil war was over, to everyone's relief.

It was an immense privilege to be in Kathmandu at that moment, celebrating with our local INF friends. We gathered together and sang, ate spicy *momos* (dumplings) with extra *achar* (tomato pickle), and then we slept very well that night.

The next week, we packed up our Himalayan home. It had always been our intention to return to Australia around that time, mainly because our eldest son was almost ready for high school. By then, Darren and the other expatriates had been able to hand over the physio training program to well-qualified, wonderful Nepali nationals. We knew the program would continue, and we were very encouraged. We said goodbye to our local friends and church community over extended meals of *dal bhat* (rice and lentils), boarded an aeroplane and returned to Australia.

§

That was a shock in itself – footpaths and straight roads and supermarkets and grandparents. There were no armed soldiers or chickens or buffalo in the bazaar. Darren quickly got a job lecturing on anatomy at the University of Sydney, which he really enjoyed, and our three sons went off to 'real' school, which they mostly enjoyed. While they were there, I adjusted to our quiet, empty house in the Blue Mountains, which was full of electricity and sunshine. I continued to write, firstly the sequel to *My Seventh Monsoon*, and then a range of other books, all packed with stories. As I did, I slowly began to see the power of honest, faith-based stories that point to Jesus amidst our ordinary days and moments. Gradually, readers began to write to me, sharing how my books had changed their lives. Some said they had renewed their hope in God, who is sovereign and good, always. Others told me that they had come to faith in Jesus while reading my books. Many said that reading the stories helped them to hold on to God's grace and mercy during their own intense struggles.

This feedback was amazing to me. As followers of Jesus, we're on a shared journey. We struggle along, with our doubts and disappointments and questions and moaning. Yet, we strive to fix our eyes on Jesus, who is faithful and good, even when we are not. Every day, to keep our eyes fixed on Jesus, we need each other's support.

One of my favourite prayers is found in Ephesians 3. Paul prays that the believers in Ephesus will be able to grasp the love of God, in all its breadth and height and wonder, 'together with all the Lord's holy people' (v. 18). Paul knew they would be able to grasp the love of God on their own, individually, as we all do, but they could grasp it so much better *together*. We need each other! We need to grasp God's truths, mercy and lavish forgiveness *together with all the Lord's holy people* – with young and old, men and women, and quirky aunts and bouncing toddlers. We need to read and understand God's truths with people who speak different languages, have different opinions, wear different clothes and live in all kinds of places we don't easily find on a map.

One of my later books became *Finding Faith*, commissioned by my publisher in the UK. It shared 13 testimonies from people around the world who had come to faith in Jesus as adults, out of other religious backgrounds. Hearing those stories was deeply encouraging to me, especially the variety of experiences and the amazing reminder that God's love and truth reach across every culture and language and people group. Another book became *The Plum Tree in the Desert*, a collection of 10 of the most encouraging stories of faith and mission in Asia and the Arab world. I loved writing that one, for Interserve, partly because it involved travel to Kyrgyzstan, China, Tibet and India! But also, the more I wrote, the more I realised the depth of encouragement we draw from each other's honest stories of faith and mission. We don't need to be in a civil war, wheelchair, Hindu kingdom or state of emergency to be able to relate to another person's life story and be pointed back to our wonderful God who has shown us grace in Christ – a God who will give us strength to face our own ongoing struggles and perplexing questions.

In 2019, I wrote a book with Feby Chan, *Walking Him Home*, about her faith story. Feby is a person of deep, intercessory prayer. In her 20s, she was employed full-time in her church in Yogyakarta, Indonesia, as a prayer intercessor. In her 30s, she was invited to Kerobokan Prison in Bali to set up a prayer ministry with the inmates. While she was there, she met Andrew Chan, an Australian man who was on death row for drug smuggling. During his early years in prison, Andrew had been transformed by God through a living relationship with Jesus Christ. Together, Feby and Andrew began a prayer ministry in the prison, and they saw God at work in wonderful, life-giving ways. They were part of a revival that God brought about amongst the inmates, and for all those years, Feby earnestly believed that Andrew would be released. She prayed fervently for him, as did many people around the world, and she believed that God could, and would, do a miracle. Andrew and Feby were engaged in early 2015 and married on 27 April 2015.

Thirty-five hours later, Andrew was executed by firing squad.

Feby's faith story is *also* about what happens in the darkness, when God doesn't do what we expect and we feel abandoned. For me, spending many months with Feby, writing her story and praying with her, touched me deeply. We all need stories like Feby's, because in *our* hard moments of doubt and despair, we are drawn back to the same God who is *still* good and loving and holy, even when we can't see it, and even when the worst things happen in our lives.

After finishing Feby's story, I had a moment of clarity. For nearly two decades, God had been giving me opportunities to write other people's faith stories. Perhaps it was his ongoing answer to my question at 12 years old: How could I love others, as Jesus had loved me, for a lifetime? How could I keep pointing other people to God's grace? The answer for me was, in part, writing other people's faith stories.

I kept going. After Feby's book, I had a new idea. What if I could collect and write *shorter* faith stories from people all around me, near and far – anyone I could find? Admittedly, I became a bit compulsive, but the faith stories were published online by *Eternity News* and Bible Society Australia, and the shorter word count meant that I could do more of them!

It turned out to be excellent timing. By then it was early 2020, and the global pandemic had begun. While everything else was unravelling around the world, I was on the phone, hearing stories of God at work and how he was drawing people to himself in Christ, throughout Australia and from 33 different countries. It was a gift to my own depleted heart. For four years, I kept interviewing everyone I could find, and I was deeply encouraged by their testimonies. I loved the honesty and vulnerability of my interviewees as they shared their struggles and answers with me. In some ways, the sheer depth of their honesty was surprising to me. In Australia, I had found that people weren't always keen to open their front doors to visitors unless their house was immaculate. And yet, here were hundreds of people opening their heart doors to me and revealing their raw, honest, messy stories, full of doubts and fears and struggles. In doing so, many of them relived moments when God had intervened in powerful ways – from the moment they decided to follow Jesus to the numerous ways that God had been at work in their lives since then.

By the end of 2023, I paused. I had written 300 honest faith stories. All of them had shaped and inspired me, and I felt privileged to have met each person and been a small part of capturing their story. I loved it. But something else happened along the way – something I hadn't expected. As well as being the listener and the conduit, I was given enormous insight into the human heart and the ways of God's Spirit. I was gifted new, tender glimpses into the lives and questions of ordinary Australians. I was brought to my knees by a far richer perspective of God's sovereignty within suffering and faith. I saw new, unexpected patterns about the ways God seemed to work in drawing people to himself, through faith in the Lord Jesus.

I decided to take a break from my frantic gathering of faith stories and share my thoughts about these perspectives and patterns with you, in a book. Even the writing process – choosing 63 stories from 300 – and putting them together in a helpful order has been a great delight to me. I hope you find it encouraging. I especially hope you enjoy the great *variety* of people and their stories – open-hearted believers from every state in Australia, overcome by the love of God in Christ. My wish is that you catch those same glimpses – how the questions we ask find their beautiful answers in Jesus. Notice the same heartwarming patterns – especially the fact that human unravelling is often part of our faith stories, and that God often works through the presence of trusted friends, as well as through his word in the Bible and the powerful work of his Holy Spirit.

Most of all, I'd love us to remember that this is God's story. He has invited us into it, through the death and resurrection of his own Son, the Lord Jesus Christ. He works in us, and in the world, to redeem and restore. As we continue to put our trust in Jesus and submit to him, God will continue to bring about his good plans and purposes in our own lives, and in the world, until he returns in glory and redeems all things. We can trust him.

'Let the redeemed of the Lord tell their story.'
(Ps 107:2)

2
The Unravelling

In the 300 stories that I collected, there was an enormous amount of variety: there was no one story, sentence, question, expression or circumstance that was the same. Every story was so unique and different – to the point that hearing each story made my heart sing with thanksgiving to God, whose ways are so far above our small understanding. God works uniquely and personally in each human life, and I was overwhelmed by God's holiness and utter love for humanity. God will act in a million different ways in our lives, according to his own sovereign purposes, to draw us to himself in Christ.

I did see some patterns in these stories, though, which will be the focus of this book, and I'm going to begin with the concept of unravelling, as it was strikingly present in many of the faith stories. If you're anything like me, you've probably experienced times of your own 'unravelling'. Sometimes it starts off as a loose thread in our lives, or an unanswerable question, or a wordless fear, or a deep ache in our belly ... and then the next minute we're standing beside a hospital bed, or feeling numb at a funeral, or experiencing an emptiness or lack of purpose, or we're waiting hopelessly for a phone call that might signal the end of the dream. Perhaps your own experience of brokenness or unravelled dreams has weighed you down so much that you have wondered whether you will ever be able to put your threads back together again.

2. The Unravelling

In a high proportion of the faith stories I collected, I noticed a correlation between personal unravelling and an openness to Jesus Christ. Of all the interviewees, 65% described deep struggles in the period prior to putting their trust in Jesus. The percentage was even higher (87%) among people who came to faith in Jesus as adults. Many people described their experiences of pain in the world and within themselves that they couldn't fix. They also spoke about grappling with questions of purpose and meaning amidst brokenness, failure, illness, abuse, depression, grief and addictions.

In some ways, it seems obvious. We can't fix our lostness or heal our burdens on our own. The gospel message tells us that we are all in need. As sinners, we are separated from God and desperately need a Saviour. When we come to God in dire need, we are amazed that Jesus' death on the cross has paid for our sins. In response, we repent and place our faith in him, longing for God to transform and heal us. As we pray, we receive God's Spirit and his promise of life-changing hope, forgiveness, purpose and peace.

But how do people describe what is usually, in reality, a convoluted process? In the past, I might have imagined that a clear gospel outline or presentation would then be followed by the hearer acknowledging their need and responding to God's grace. And while an understanding of the gospel is absolutely crucial, what I actually observed in these stories was that human unravelling, when acknowledged, was the thing that preceded faith in Jesus. Acknowledging brokenness, emptiness or lostness was the key to a person opening themselves to Jesus Christ, allowing God to reveal his truth to them in countless ways.

I personally find this observation both freeing and encouraging, particularly regarding my unbelieving friends and relations. I have many of these, as I'm sure you do too. I love them deeply and long for them to know the truth and beauty of Jesus. I long for them to experience the peace and wholeness that comes from receiving God's forgiveness. I pray for them daily, and fervently. Sometimes, I imagine that if I were to explain the gospel to them, once again, in a neat, riveting little conversation, then they would immediately respond to Jesus in faith, on the spot.

Interestingly, after 300 conversations, very few people described one neat, riveting little conversation that suddenly illuminated the whole gospel truth. Very few even described one brilliant sermon that convinced them of complete, robust theological ideas that immediately drew them to faith in Jesus.

However, the great majority *did* describe their unravelling as the place where it began. Sometimes it was acute unravelling in a certain moment. At other times, it was long decades of ongoing struggle. It makes me wonder about my own early unravelling. As I said earlier, I was a very quiet 12-year-old, constantly worried that my words and thoughts would be wrong. Perhaps it was partly because a few years prior, my father had left our family home. Maybe I withdrew into myself, wordlessly, to prevent further likelihood of loss or repercussions. Either way, I unravelled, and I knew it.

The truth is that in every human life, there is or there will be an unravelling sooner or later. We will all admit that something is not right in our world and that something is definitely not right in our own hearts. We're in a mess, and we can't fix it, no matter how hard we try. In that acknowledgement, we hunger for answers and long for hope. We dream of light in the fury of our darkness.

2. The Unravelling

I'd love to share a few examples of stories of unravelling with you. There are so many examples to choose from. Some of the stories I have chosen highlight specific distress or questions the person faced. Others describe relationship breakdowns, external struggles or overwhelming trauma. In all cases, acknowledging their unravelling ultimately led them to find hope in Jesus.

I'll start with our friend **Scott**. He and his wife Janelle arrived at our local church in the Blue Mountains early in 2020. Over the next few years, over many shared meals and Bible studies, Scott told us about his experience of unravelling. The following is a summary of his story. Interestingly, Scott's unravelling was preceded by significant worldly success.

> 'I had a heart attack when I was 17. I'd been playing tennis at a high level ... and I was in the Queensland Championships. After the match, I went home, and I jumped into our backyard pool. My heart went into spasm, and I woke up in the cardiac ward at Brisbane Hospital. It was full of old guys who were about to die. One of them said to me, "What are you doing here?"
>
> This experience gave me a new perspective on life. After 12 months, I was allowed to play tennis again ... and I threw myself into everything.
>
> For the next 10 years, I tried to be the best I could possibly be, in every part of life – in tennis and in work. I got involved in a really successful company doing building design. I bought a house and an MG. I moved to Sydney to start up a Sydney branch. We were turning over six million dollars a year.

It was ridiculous. I was only 27 years old, and I had all that responsibility and stress.

Eventually, it led to a mental and physical breakdown. I lost everything, and I became homeless at age 28. I moved onto my mate's lounge. I slowly realised that I was not in control, and I never had been, no matter how high I'd climbed the tree.

A few months later, I started asking everyone I knew about the meaning of life. What did they believe in? Where was the book? How did they know? I was hungry for meaning. I met Janelle, through a friend. We went on a date, and I told her I was trying to figure out the meaning of life. She told me she was a Christian, and she invited me to church.

I said, "No way! I'd never go to church. They're a bunch of hypocrites."

We were very honest with each other. A few months later, she invited me to a carol singalong. I went, and afterwards I talked to the minister for two hours. He invited me to lunch, and we kept meeting, weekly. We started reading the Gospel of Mark together. But it didn't really click.

Then he asked me to do a course called Christianity Explained. I said I wasn't ready to make a commitment, but I went anyway. We got up to the page on condemnation. I can still remember it. There was a black-and-white line drawing of a group of people hiding their faces from the glory of God.

Suddenly, I was an absolute, blubbering, out-of-control mess on the floor. It happened in a split second. I was stripped bare before a holy God. It was an absolutely powerful encounter

> with the Holy Spirit. I became aware of my sin for the first time, and I totally understood the grace of God – the incredible mercy of God – that he should forgive me and save me, through Jesus. It was beautiful!
>
> Everything changed in an instant. I read the Bible all the way through, twice! And I felt peace, every time I prayed. It transcended understanding, like it says in Philippians 4:6–7! I love that verse about God's peace. It says God's peace "will guard your hearts and your minds in Christ Jesus." I can't tell you what God has done in the years since then. Before I became a Christian, I'd always been anxious and striving. I couldn't cope with uncertainty. But now, I love uncertainty. God is changing me! It's been exponentially better than anything I could have imagined. Janelle and I got married. We had two children, and we went off to Cambodia, as missionaries. Even now, in tough times, uncertainty doesn't faze me. I know that God is sovereign. And he's got it!'

It's a wonderful testimony, isn't it? I love Scott's honesty regarding his specific unravelling. For him, it began with a heart attack at 17, followed by a decade of striving for outer success, which left him unsatisfied despite reaching the top. Scott eventually broke down and became homeless, sleeping on a friend's lounge, overwhelmed with questions. He unravelled. During that time of stress and emptiness, he finally admitted to himself that he had never been in control. He needed answers and he searched everywhere. I love that God was guiding his steps all the way along. Scott met Janelle and then a minister, and they read through the Gospel of Mark together. It didn't make sense to him until the moment the Holy Spirit worked powerfully in his heart, stripping him bare before a holy God. Scott realised he was a sinner deserving condemnation, yet he was offered grace. He understood that he should hide his face from the glory of God, yet he was offered life and complete forgiveness through Jesus' death and resurrection. God answered Scott's deepest questions in his timing, after the unravelling, using people like Janelle and the minister.

I particularly appreciate the way Scott described his transformation over time. He used to be someone regularly fazed by uncertainty, but now he can slow down and rest in God's sovereignty and goodness. The wonderful thing is that this is true for each of us at every stage of life, including today. Scott's faith story reminds *me* to look to Jesus for true rest and peace in my current tasks, challenges, deadlines and concerns. We are not in control, but God is, and we can pray. *Lord, show us your mercy again, as you did for Scott.*

§

In the midst of Scott's unravelling, he admitted truthfully and vulnerably that he wasn't in control. He was broken and fragile. Unravelling tends to do that, doesn't it? Our times of stress and questioning often force us to acknowledge our vulnerabilities, or our deepest emotions that we usually try to keep hidden. With that in mind, meet **Kaz**. Like Scott, Kaz described her unravelling to me, but in her case, it was due to a combination of unexpected family needs and bereavement. As she unravelled, Kaz admitted truthfully that she felt a deep sense of shame.

> 'I had a very hard time five years ago. We lost my mum, aunty and daughter's best friend, all in the space of three months. It

was too much for my daughter. She became addicted to ice … and during her addiction I took care of my grandson.

It was really hard. My husband and I were suddenly looking after a three-year-old boy, as well as managing my retail shop in Melbourne. And because of my business, I didn't want other people to know about my daughter's drug addiction. I felt the stigma and shame of it, and I didn't want to tell anyone. Eventually, I was in such a mess that I went to the doctor, and I told him what was going on.

He gave me a piece of paper with a lady's name on it. She was a mental health clinician and she counselled me for three days. She said that we can't control what other people say, think and do. It's not our responsibility. We are not in control of our loved one's addiction. She also helped me to network with services that would help my daughter when she was ready.

But halfway through that year, I also started going to church. I think I was searching for some sort of calm through my massive storm. My parents had been Christians and invited me to church, but I always said no. I used to say that it wasn't my thing. But when I started looking after my grandson, I started going to his (Christian) school assemblies. I really liked the songs the children sang. They were pretty hip for Christian music. I'd go home and find them on the internet, and I'd put them on the playlist on my phone. I even changed my radio to Vision Christian Media.

I decided to go to the church on the school grounds. The first time I went, I met a gentleman who had known my parents. He knew all about their faith journey and he shared it with me. It was fantastic! It made me feel so much closer to them.

But that first year, everywhere I went, the same verse would pop up. It was John 3:16. "For God so loved the world that he gave his one and only Son, that whoever believes in him shall not perish but have eternal life."

That verse was everywhere! I'd never heard it before. I'd never read the Bible before … but it was telling me something. I saw it on the back of the church newsletter, then up on the screen after the sermon, then on a billboard near our local restaurant, and then in a book for parents of addicts. Every time I saw it, I cried. God was telling me that it was okay and that he loved me, and that he had given up his Son Jesus for me.

I believed it. I'm so thankful to God. He has been with me all the time; I just didn't know him.

I've also come to realise that God uses us to help others. My journey through my daughter's addiction has let me connect with so many parents to help them through their child's addiction. I have a red couch at the back of my shop, and people always come and sit to share their journeys. With God's grace, I am able to help them.

My family has also been restored. My daughter is now three years clean. It was because of my journey that I was able to help her get the help she needed. How amazing is it to have my God in my life!'

2. The Unravelling

There's so much to love and relate to in Kaz's faith story. She admitted that she was in an awful mess and she couldn't hide from it or run away. She felt the shame and stigma of addiction, as well as the helplessness of a parent who dearly loves an adult child in pain. She longed for calm within her storm.

Amazingly, in Kaz's unravelling, God provided for her in so many ways. There was the helpful doctor who introduced her to a counsellor, the counsellor who provided much-needed advice, and the worship music at her grandson's school that touched her heart. She felt prompted to go to church, where she immediately met a man who knew her parents. Best of all, God allowed the wonderful truth of John 3:16 to keep appearing in her life. I love that Kaz had never heard of it before and that God used it so powerfully, drawing her to faith in Jesus. Additionally, I love how Kaz's transformation over time turned into a longing and availability to help others. I can clearly picture her and her comfy red lounge in the back of her shop, inviting customers to sit there and share. I'd love to sit on it!

Kaz's story also challenges me and makes me question: Am *I* deliberately noticing the way God has been providing for me today, in the form of friends, contacts, music and Scripture? Am I able to see God's generous provision even amidst pain? Am I faithfully channelling the lessons I have learned during the unravelling years to help others? *Lord, please help each of us look to you in our pain, and please help each of us to thank you for your provision, becoming people who overflow with gratitude.*

§

For some of us, our unravelling is not a short or momentary thing. It might instead be a lifetime of pain, distress or questions. For others, it can take the form of quiet disappointment. **Bec and Memo** are examples. They shared with me their story of a marriage that was slowly drifting apart.

> 'We met when I (Bec) was 18 and Memo was 27. He had a Mexican background, and we met through a Mexican dance performance group. We hit it off straight away. We got married, and we had four children. But it was when our first child was small that our marriage began to drift. I was struggling with that, and one day, some Jehovah's Witnesses knocked at our door. I actually invited them in. I was lonely and depressed, so I said, "Come in and have a cup of tea."
>
> They kept coming back, every week, for a year. We read the Bible together, and it actually got Memo and me interested in the Bible for the first time. Before that, I hadn't thought much about faith or the Bible. I probably thought there was a God. Memo was the same. He had a Catholic background, but he had questions. What are we here for? He was even searching for answers in outer space.
>
> After a year, the Jehovah's Witnesses asked us to come to their church, but we said no … and then we never saw them again.
>
> Some years later, though, things got really bad for us in our marriage. We were on the verge of splitting up. At the time, I knew that our neighbour was a Christian, and she went to church. I had the feeling that I'd like to take our kids to church. So we went to her church, on and off, for a year. Nothing really sunk in. But one day, someone at her church gave us a leaflet about a weekend marriage course. She'd heard that we were having marriage problems.

I showed the leaflet to Memo, and he said, "You go. You're the one with the problems."

But the next day, Memo changed his mind. He said, "I'll go if you want to go."

We went to the marriage weekend. The first session on the Friday night ripped us apart. We fought afterwards. We pulled the two beds apart so that we wouldn't have to sleep near each other. The next morning, we decided that we wouldn't stay at the course. We would tell the organisers and leave.

But we looked everywhere, and we couldn't find the organisers. So, we said to each other that we'd just listen to the next session and then we'd leave.

But during that session, God started revealing himself to us. We were hearing about how God is the answer to our marriage. The speaker said that in a marriage, you need Jesus in the middle, like the third strand of a braid – the one you can't see. You can't do it on your own, without him. And he said that the Bible has the answers – that Jesus died for our sins and there was an enemy dividing us. Memo said that he'd never understood it before. But it became real for us both, right then in that moment. It felt like everything was making sense. We cried a lot that day! We came to Christ together. It was instantaneous!

We kept talking about it on the way home in the car. We couldn't wait to tell everyone! It was so urgent. From that day on, we've never stopped reading the Bible together. And we've changed. Our family has changed.

> We started going to Mexico regularly, to help in an orphanage. Then we thought we'd go and serve long-term, but the doors didn't open, so instead, we now work with a refugee ministry in Sydney. We also open our home up to Aboriginal teens from the Northern Territory on school scholarships.
>
> For both of us, our favourite Bible passage is in Acts 9. Saul was nearing Damascus and "suddenly a light from heaven flashed around him." Saul heard the voice of Jesus, and later "something like scales fell from Saul's eyes, and he could see again". That's exactly how it felt for us. It was like scales fell from our eyes!'

Isn't that great? Scales fell from Bec and Memo's eyes, and they could both see the truth of Jesus clearly. But once again, it started with unravelling. Bec described her loneliness and disconnection within a marriage that was drifting apart. Memo had questions. I find it interesting that their journey to faith in Jesus began with a Jehovah's Witness at the door and a neighbour. God used those interactions, and both Bec and Memo began to read the Bible and attend church. Even so, the unravelling continued unabated. They agreed to go to the marriage course, but even there, they pushed their beds firmly apart and were determined to leave.

I find it amazing that sometimes our entire stories are impacted by a single moment. The next morning, Bec and Memo couldn't find the organiser, so they had to stay at the course … and then they heard that Jesus died for their sins. God revealed himself to both of them, and scales fell from their eyes in an instant. How wonderful!

2. The Unravelling

Of course, there are so many stories where a person's journey to faith is slow, taking place over many years, or very disjointed. Married couples do not always come to faith in Jesus together. In fact, there are many stories of decades of uncertainty and fervent prayer in between. There are no guarantees. But for Bec and Memo, it was instantaneous and together. I think we need to hear and rejoice in every kind of story. The slow stories remind me of God's longer perspective. He is patient with us, not wanting anyone to perish. The instantaneous stories remind me that God can reveal himself to us in a rush if he wants to. Our responses can be filled with urgency. Jesus is the Lord of all, and it's time to respond!

I love the way Bec and Memo responded quickly. They were cut to the heart and both acknowledged Jesus as Lord. They read the Bible together, went to Mexico, and helped out in a refugee ministry. Of course, it doesn't always work out that way. But when it does, we see again that following Jesus isn't an optional, 'one day I'll get around to that' category. He is Lord of all today! Let's pray for a similar sense of gospel urgency in our lives and decisions today. *Lord, please quicken our hearts as we respond to you. Fill us with a new sense of urgency, we pray.*

§

Here is another observation after gathering 300 faith stories: there is a type of unravelling that is largely unseen. It is quiet and internal, even subconscious. It may look like outer confidence, indifference or worldly bluster, but underneath, there are questions and inconsistencies. Sometimes, those internal inconsistencies are only verbally acknowledged years later, in the light of the gospel. That was certainly the case for **Mike**.

'I grew up in a secular home in suburban Australia where religion was categorically rejected – it was seen as a crutch, and people of faith were derided as morally deviant hypocrites. I remember, as a teenager, I wrote poetry mocking belief in God. My mother threw enough profanity at religious door knockers to make even a sailor blush.

Many years later, however, I was invited to church by a colleague in the military. I went along out of boredom, wanting to do something different. I thought most churches were filled with moralising geriatrics. I was very, very wrong.

I began to read the New Testament for myself. The Jesus I encountered was far different from the deluded, radical or even mythical character described to me. This Jesus – the Jesus of history – was real. He touched upon things that cut close to my heart, especially as I pondered the meaning of human existence. I was struck by the early church's testimony to Jesus: in Christ's death, God has vanquished evil, and by his resurrection, he has brought life and hope to all.

When I crossed from unbelief to belief, all the pieces suddenly began to fit together. I had always felt a strange unease about my unbelief. I had an acute suspicion that there might be something more, something transcendent, but I also knew that I was told not to think that. I "knew" that ethics were nothing more than aesthetics, a mere word game for things I liked and disliked. I felt conflicted when my heart ached over the injustice and cruelty in the world.

> As faith grew from seeds of doubt, I came upon a whole new world that, for the first time, actually made sense to me. My life changed immediately. I wasn't always on the town with the guys looking for a good time in bars and clubs. I cleaned up my life, my language and my attitudes to many things. I took to reading the Bible daily, and I started reading about Christian theology and learning about the lives of important men and women in church history.
>
> I was very touched by Galatians 2:20, "I have been crucified with Christ and I no longer live, but Christ lives in me. The life I now live in the body, I live by faith in the Son of God, who loved me and gave himself for me." That verse has always remained with me wherever I've been, in the good times and the bad.
>
> To this day, I do not find faith stifling or constricting. Rather, faith has been liberating and transformative for me. It has opened a constellation of meaning, beauty, hope and life that I had been indoctrinated to deny. It has compelled my lifelong quest to know, study and teach about the one whom Christians called Lord.'

Mike's testimony is wonderful and unique. I appreciate his description of the liberating, transformative life of following Jesus, offering a new constellation of meaning, beauty, hope and life. But do you also notice the nod he gave to his internal inconsistencies in previous years when he mocked faith as a younger person? Mike admitted to a strange unease. He felt conflicted and had an acute suspicion that there was something more. Outwardly, he was confident and mocking, yet inwardly, his heart ached, especially regarding ethics, justice and transcendence. It's a different kind of unravelling – a very quiet kind, the kind we try to ignore, justify or reduce. But those inconsistencies and questions will continue to whisper in the quiet of the night until we are faced with the reality of the person of Jesus Christ, and all our thoughts are flung wide open.

Mike's story also makes me thankful again for the friends and acquaintances who are often such a key part of our testimonies. We will consider these relationships more in chapter 3, but for now, it's good to acknowledge Mike's military colleague who invited him to church. Perhaps that particular invitation required more courage than we might imagine, in the face of possible mockery or derision.

Even more than that, Mike's story causes me to pause and wonder again at the indisputable, life-giving, historical reality of the person of Jesus, whose death vanquished evil and whose resurrection brought life-giving hope to all. May this Jesus continue to compel us and flood us with the courage we need today to love and serve our neighbours and the world. *Lord, we ask you to fill us again with the sheer wonder of your presence and redeeming work, that we might be compelled to share it with the people in front of us.*

§

Sometimes, the human unravelling we experience occurs when our expectations aren't met in the way we imagined. I'm sure you've also had times of deep disappointment, perhaps fuelled by very high expectations. Life can often be disappointing. For those of us who have perhaps spent many years preparing (or longing) to be a spouse, a parent, a university student, a successful employee, a well-known creative artist, or anything at all, the reality of those achievements is not always blissful or what we imagined. We may then wonder: What is the point of all this? For **Ellie**, her disappointments and questions occurred relatively early in her life, at age 18.

> 'Throughout my high school years in Sydney, my aim in life was to make people like me. I wanted to do well at school, have good friends and go to the right parties. By year 12, I was doing pretty well at all that! My teachers liked me, I had good friends and my parents were pleased with me. In fact, it felt like I could people-please my way into most relationships.
>
> Then, halfway through my final year of school, I went on a Crusaders study camp. My plan was to study, hang out with my friends and ignore all the Jesus stuff. Up until then, my friendships had always been transactional. It's how we operated. I'll lend you my geography notes and you'll invite me to your party on Saturday night.
>
> So, I went on the study camp and approached it much the same way. But when I got there, I heard the gospel presented clearly for the first time and saw people living it out in sacrificial, not transactional, love. They said that Jesus was their Lord, and they lived like he was. I could see they were living a coherent life. They treated me differently. They were actually interested in me personally, and for the first time, it wasn't transactional. They just wanted to get to know me. I kept thinking … but don't you want to know who I'm friends with, what I'm good at or why it's worth getting to know me? They didn't.
>
> After the camp, I went away thinking that I needed to figure out who this Jesus was. Perhaps he's not as dismissible as I

thought. Back then, I had two friends at school who were Christians, so I asked them if I could go to church with them. They said yes, and I went to church and started to piece together a picture of Jesus. He was holy and good and powerful. But I still didn't think I needed him. I was doing well in life, and I didn't need Jesus.

Then I finished my HSC [Higher School Certificate], and I went to schoolies on the Gold Coast, Queensland. It was meant to be the pinnacle of my life so far. I could tick off all the things that I'd been working so hard for and give myself a pat on the back.

But it wasn't all great. If the pinnacle of my life was being in Surfers Paradise, surrounded by drunk people who were vomiting in the corridors, then maybe my pinnacle wasn't all that it was cracked up to be.

At the same time, the Red Frogs came and knocked on my door. They're the Christian chaplains who minister at schoolies. I invited them in because I still had questions about Jesus. On Sunday, I went to church with them. At church, there was a testimony, and afterwards, we were invited to trust in Jesus and to pray.

That's when I decided that I didn't want to run from God's love anymore. I realised, during that year, why Jesus came. We're not good enough for God. Even though I could people-please my way into most people's good books, I couldn't do that with God. I did need Jesus after all, because he is the only one good enough for God.

> The big thing that has changed for me after coming to faith in Jesus has been in my relationships. I've found, over time, that I have a new capacity to love people – not transactionally. I can love people because God has already loved me. It's been a big change, and I've had slow realisations. Even in Christian ministry, we don't meet with people because we think they're going to respond to Jesus. We meet with people because we love them, regardless. "This is love: not that we loved God, but that he loved us and sent his Son as an atoning sacrifice for our sins. Dear friends, since God so loved us, we also ought to love one another" (1 John 4:10-11).
>
> I have to keep learning this! My temptation is always to go back to a transactional mindset. But every day, I can love people because love comes from God. Every day, I need a fountain of love and I know that it only comes from Jesus.'

I find it interesting that Ellie heard about Jesus at church and saw his impact on her friends at camp, but she still didn't think she needed him. She was doing well in life, grades and relationships and felt she didn't need Jesus. Then she went to schoolies and faced the emptiness of her life. The disappointment of her supposed pinnacle not being great at all led her to admit that she did need Jesus. Only he is good enough. Ellie responded to the gospel of grace. Like Ellie, we all live in a world pushing us toward self-actualisation and self-fulfilment in a myriad of ways at every life stage. Yet many of the things we set up as pinnacles in life will turn out to be hollow as we approach them. In remarkable contrast, as we approach Jesus and know him more and more, his glorious goodness, holiness and words of hope will become brighter the closer we get.

It's also true, as Ellie noted, that a transactional mindset is at the heart of our current society, often without us even noticing it. Teenagers may trade study notes for party invitations, but similarly, as adults, we may trade time, affection, money, resources, friendships, and so on, for all sorts of defined and ill-defined benefits. Sometimes those benefits turn out to be less than desirable, and we are quick to defriend, malign, or at least leave a scathing review on a public website.

And then there is the stunning gospel message. God loved us while we were sinners. He loved us before we knew him and certainly before we loved him. Amazingly, as we understand and receive God's love, we can love him and others in return. I find it especially encouraging that Ellie saw glimpses of non-transactional love in her faith-filled friends at the study camp. May those friends read her faith story and feel encouraged today! May we also *be* those kinds of friends, whose lives are visibly consistent to anyone nearby, even those who may be watching without us knowing. *Lord, please fill us again with your astounding, non-transactional love, that we may also be people who can pour it out, unreservedly.*

§

A key aspect of human unravelling is the moment when we are faced with the core of ourselves: that we are unworthy and unable. We are sinners in need of a Saviour. We are broken and weak, and totally incapable of saving ourselves. We need saving! In talking to 300 people, I have found that that particular realisation takes many forms and is expressed in many different words. Often, it's a realisation that grows deeper and richer over time. I have often heard it said that the closer we get to Jesus, the more we realise our unworthiness and absolute lack without him. Jesus is our righteousness! I'd like you to meet **Angelina**, who realised she was a sinner at age 57.

> 'I was a New Age nomad for 10 years. It was after my husband left me in my 40s. He took all of his belongings and the car, and he left me a note and $40. We had five children aged five, 10, 12, 15 and 17.
>
> But I gradually found work, and the children grew up and left home. That was when I became fascinated by other things. I had no moral compass at all. I'd always been interested in Eastern religions, so I began to read lots of New Age books, and they said we find god within. They said that we become god. I was so deceived, but I wanted more, and I was never satisfied. I can't even tell you all the terrible things I did in those years.
>
> Until one day, I was on my way to Perth, camping. Two people came up to me and asked me where I was going. I said I was on my way to Perth and that my car wasn't going very well. The lady asked me if I would like them to pray for me. I said yes, and they did. The lady started praying in tongues. I had never heard it before and I was immediately fascinated. The next day, I drove into Adelaide and I couldn't stop thinking about it. I found my way to a church, and I asked the pastor about speaking in tongues. The pastor spoke to me about Jesus. He talked about sin. I hadn't thought about sin for a long time. I suddenly realised I was a sinner and I needed saving.

> I got the revelation straight away. Jesus died for me, and all my sins were forgiven. I prayed the sinner's prayer, and I prayed to receive the Holy Spirit.
>
> It was amazing! I was 57 years old, and God made me all new. I started reading the Gospels, and the truth inserted in my mind, little by little. It seemed incredible that an almighty God who had a trillion things to attend to: stars and planets, and billions of souls to care about ... that he would pay attention to one sorry, sinful soul like me ... but he did. And Psalm 18:19 became my life's verse: "He ... rescued me because he delighted in me." After that, I spent 23 years in the Middle East as part of a prayer ministry.'

Isn't that amazing? After 10 years of a certain wild kind of life, Angelina was stopped in her tracks by God. She heard people praying in strange tongues and was so intrigued that she tracked down a church pastor, who talked to her about Jesus. Angelina suddenly realised she was a sinner in need of saving. God used her natural curiosity and sense of intrigue to draw her to himself. Previously, those same tendencies had taken her down a New Age path, but then she was confronted with her need and the truth of Jesus. Her curiosity turned to repentance and confession before a holy God. No other religion or worldview evokes that kind of response. No other religion provides the answer. Our debts have been paid by the sinless Lord Jesus, who died on a cross in our place.

I especially love the immediate transformation in Angelina's life. As she began to understand the love of God for her, she responded with urgency. She went off to the Middle East and spent 23 years as part of a prayer ministry. She has so many stories!

May we also find time today to consider the enormity of the gospel truth that our almighty God, who has a trillion things to attend to, pays attention to small, sorry souls like us. He hears our prayers, restores us and sends us out. *Thank you, Lord Jesus, for this truth – that you care about and redeem small, sorry sinners like us. Help us to respond to your truth again today.*

§

We've touched on a variety of types of unravelling, and every kind reminds us that something is not right in this world, and indeed, something is not right in our own hearts. But of all the circumstances that cause us to unravel, perhaps the most profound is facing death – either our own death or the loss of a loved one. It's the one awful, unavoidable truth, and it brings us to our knees every time. Let's hear from **Tim**.

> 'I didn't grow up in a Christian household, and we didn't go to church. My dad's side was quite religious, but my mum's side were atheists.
>
> When I was 25, my father passed away quite suddenly. He was only 60 years old. I loved my father. He and I got on like a house on fire. We never argued. He was my rock growing up. And then he was gone.
>
> For anyone, death is not a nice thing at all. For me, I blamed God. I felt like God had taken my dad from us, and I was angry at him.
>
> My life went pretty badly after that, pretty quickly. After Dad passed away, my mum became unwell, and she was hospitalised for a significant period of time.

Back then, I was working for a big, global organisation in Adelaide. They offered me a role in Sydney, but I said no because I wanted to look after my mum. Then a year later, they offered me a role again and my mum said I should go.

It was a big move! I was suddenly living in a small apartment in Erskineville, Sydney, without my community. It was my second rock bottom in quick time.

Not long after that, one of my cousins asked me to come to church. I said okay. I had nothing to lose. I was still angry at God for taking my father away, and I wanted answers.

The first time I went to church, I felt very uncomfortable. I didn't fit in, so I thought I might go and find a different church. Over the next few months, I went to six different churches. Each time, I felt intimidated, judged and answerless!

Then I was introduced to Winnie. She asked me to come to her church and I said okay. It was church number seven. The speaker there preached on the book of Job and suffering. That started the juices flowing. Afterwards, Winnie gave me some audio cassettes on Job, and I listened to them after work.

The following Sunday I went back to her church. I grabbed the pastor after the service, and we went and sat in a quiet space. He asked me some questions and the tears started flowing. I told him about my dad. It was a very emotional time. I had normally been a functional, practical sort of bloke. But I realised God's love for me was unconditional, and I fell in love with him right then. I accepted Jesus. I realised he was my rock! I had idolised my dad and lost him, but there was Someone even more loving and more powerful than my dad.

> That was the start of it. Afterwards, I read the Gospel of Mark with a bloke from church. I married Winnie! I kept working in the corporate world – 21 years all up. I loved it. Then, in my early 40s, I got on board with City Bible Forum to help connect the gospel with people in the workplace. It's been a big change from the corporate world, but a real joy! A key verse for me has always been 1 Corinthians 13:4–7. "Love is patient, love is kind. It does not envy, it does not boast, it is not proud ... It always protects, always trusts, always hopes, always perseveres." That's the unconditional love we receive from God, and that's the love we get to share!'

For all of us who have stood at the funeral of a dearly loved friend or family member, we can relate to Tim and his pain. Like Tim, we have felt that unbearable anguish and numbness. We have poured out tears, questions and even anger. The reality of death is the worst kind of indicator that something is tragically wrong in our broken world and in our hearts. Yet, within all of that, Tim's questions and searching led him to come to know his heavenly Father, who was truly more loving and powerful than he could ever imagine.

Tim's testimony also reminds me of the same pattern mentioned in Mike's story. So often, God puts the right people in our lives at the right time. Tim's cousin invited him to church. The answers weren't immediately obvious, and it took seven trips to seven churches before Tim heard a sermon on Job and suffering, connected with the pastor after church and prayed with him. Let's thank God today for the way he perseveres with us and provides beautiful answers, even within our grief and endless questions. *Lord, we thank you today for the way you soften our hearts and gently heal us, even in our hardest moments. Thank you that you understand suffering and that you bore our pain for us.*

§

Let's read one more example of unravelling. At least half-a-dozen people told me that they came to faith in Jesus after a major road accident. They described driving along happily, and then suddenly, a collision changed their lives. They found themselves seriously injured, in the hospital and shocked by the fact that they had been mere inches away from death. This is **Allan**'s story. He's a lovely, kind-hearted man in his late 60s.

> 'I grew up in a little town called Woodenbong, on the border of New South Wales and Queensland. There were five of us kids, and I was the eldest. My mother was a Christian, and she sent us to Sunday school. But after school, I drifted away from church. I got work as a labourer, and later in banking. I moved 84 times! Then I got out of the bank and started truck driving. I was living in Dunedoo, next to my sister and brother-in-law's property.
>
> In 1985, I was driving a semitrailer down a hill towards Caroona, west of Quirindi. Rounding a corner, the truck jumped out of gear and then landed upside down in a ditch. The cabin caught on fire and the flames covered my legs. The cabin was crushed, and I was trapped inside. People arrived on the scene, but it took two hours to get me out. A passing truck driver had a fire extinguisher, and a local doctor hit me with morphine while I was still in the cabin.
>
> I made it to Tamworth Hospital, with a police escort. It was one of those God things. The best possible orthopaedic surgeon

was nearby, and he came in. I had multiple fractures in my legs and arms, and serious burns to my legs, back, arms and hands. They amputated both my legs below my hips. They were burnt beyond saving. If they hadn't removed my legs, I would have been dead.

I was in hospital for six months. At first, it was a 50/50 chance I'd survive. But I'm stubborn. I was 31, and I was the fittest I'd ever been. My mother got three prayer chains going. The Anglican chaplain visited me. I'd be lying there, legs missing, both arms broken, propped up on pillows … and he would sit beside me. I could talk to him. He knew about trucks, so we'd talk about trucks. Then, we talked about other things. I knew if there was anything I needed, I would be able talk to him. The head nurse was also a Christian, and I had a lot of Christian visitors. That's how it started.

I started to see that God had kept me alive. I realised God was real. There were so many coincidences. He was right there at the accident. I knew that God was with me, and he hadn't finished with me yet.

After rehab, and some time with my parents, I went back home to Dunedoo, living by myself. I had two prosthetic legs by then and my arm was still in plaster, but I worked around things and managed the cooking and cleaning. I bought a car with hand controls. Then I went back to working on the farm – with two prosthetic legs and two sticks.

In the meantime, I became more and more involved with the local church. The minister was very good. I started a

> correspondence course through a Bible college, and I became a leader on Walk to Emmaus retreat weekends. I was drawing closer to God and trusting Jesus with my decisions. Within three years, I was an elder in the church. Then, at age 49, I met and married Anne! We've had 20 wonderful years together. I'm so grateful to God.
>
> Every year since the accident, I've had a second birthday on the date of my accident. I want to give thanks to God! I know that he saved me, and he still has things for me to do. Nowadays, I'm a leader in the church; I preach when needed, lead communion and operate the computer at church. I help people out in our retirement village with their tech issues.
>
> My favourite verse is Philippians 4:13: "I can do all this through him who gives me strength." I know it's God who gets me through. A sense of humour also helps! I also know that if God was there at the time of the accident, then he'll be here today and in the future. We can trust him!'

Allan's unravelling was certainly severe, yet his response was so open-hearted. He was receptive to the truth of God's presence with him, the chaplain who visited him and the gospel of grace. As God enabled and changed him, Allan became open to the needs of those around him. For decades, he and his wife Anne have faithfully served the people in their community in Lithgow. Meeting Allan and Anne recently on a sunny day in Oberon was a delight for Darren and me. They both regaled us with their stories.

Allan's story makes me thankful for the way God works, especially at our worst moments when we hit rock bottom. None of us ask for

2. The Unravelling

times of unravelling. We don't wish for grief, calamity or disaster. We'd prefer not to face disappointment, sadness, questions, breakups or shame. But the truth is that we will all unravel at some point, and it may go on for decades. We live in a world, and a wider story, that is also slowly unravelling. Even as our society pushes for more individual self-fulfilment, the answers are not forthcoming. Indeed, it appears that the emotional and spiritual needs around us are worsening.

But there is a wonderful truth in the fury of our darkness. As we come to God and admit that we are broken, sinful and needy, and cannot save ourselves – as we cry out to God, he hears us. The God of all comfort is present, drawing us to himself in Christ and lavishing grace on us, which is astounding. As the Scriptures say in Ephesians 1: 'In him we have redemption through his blood, the forgiveness of sins, in accordance with the riches of God's grace that he lavished on us' (vv. 7–8a). I pray today that in each of our stories of unravelling, we will notice God's lavish grace and his precious arms of love around us ... and respond to them.

3
Trusted friends

Here's another thing I have noticed in 300 faith stories: in the vast majority of them, new believers mentioned a friend or key contact who was part of their faith journey. This friend was usually prayerful, trustworthy and present at the right time. Sometimes the friend invited them to a Christian gathering, as in the case of Scott, Ellie and Mike. Other times, the friend prayed for them, as seen in the stories of Angelina and Tim. At times, the friend brought practical care and comfort or spoke words of truth, life and encouragement at exactly the right time, as in the case of Allan.

This is very encouraging! We all have friends, and we all *are* friends to many people in our circles. We may not always feel like we have the right gospel words at the right time, but we can all pray, comfort and be present. We can be trustworthy, available, supportive and welcoming. When I think back to my own childhood, I remember the influence of my new friend at age 12. She invited me to the Christian group at high school, and I went. But it was much more than that single invitation. We were genuine friends. We hung out at each other's houses, talked on the phone till all hours, made sparkly costumes for school dances, and laughed and cried together. She was a key part of my teenage years, so of course I went with her wherever she went. In addition, I slowly got to know her extended family, who were such a fun, loving group, especially her mum, who was like a mother hen. She always invited me to stay longer, eat whatever food they were eating and join in the general mayhem because there was always more than enough food and mayhem to go around.

I wonder if you've had a similar experience, looking back? Were there key people or friends in your life before you came to faith in Jesus? Did any of those friends or family members contribute to your deeper understanding of the gospel and your subsequent decision to follow Jesus?

§

I'd love to share with you a few more examples from the 300 faith stories as an encouragement. There are so many aspects to trusted friendship, and God uses all of them. Sometimes, the person is a relatively recent friend, like in the case of **Corey**, who made a new friend at high school. In Corey's case, his new friend also happened to be the local pastor's son, and he was remarkably persistent.

> 'My identity was always tied up in my sporting ability. I was pretty good at soccer, and I played at different high levels … so if the game went well, I'd feel good about myself … and if I stuffed up, my self-worth dropped. I'd feel like I wasn't good enough.
>
> At the same time, our family used to go to church, so I knew that God was real, but I had a sense that being a Christian meant following the rules, and ticking the boxes, and doing the right thing. If I did everything right, and pleased God, and followed his laws, then I could earn his favour and go to heaven. That's what I thought. Also, on the other hand, if I

didn't do well, then God (and others) wouldn't want to know me. Maybe it was a bit like soccer.

Then a new guy rocked up at high school. He joined our tight group of sporty guys. He said that he'd moved into the area because his dad was the new pastor at the local church. I'd never met a Christian at high school, and I'd never told anyone that I went to church. But he just shared it openly. Then he asked me if I wanted to come to his church.

I said no at first. I thought that I had enough church in my life – I used to go once every six weeks … and thought it was enough to please God. But then he must have asked me 20 times, and after a while, I said yes … mainly to shut him up.

I remember walking into his church for the first time and feeling something quite different. I was greeted by lots of different people, and we had supper together. It was like I was loved for who I was, rather than for being good enough. Then his dad started preaching on the Sermon on the Mount. The message was that God desires our hearts more than external acts. I needed a whole new heart. I needed to stop trying to fix my heart myself, and actually submit to Jesus.

I remember sitting in that place and praying. I realised for the first time that Christ died for me while I was still a sinner. Paul says in Romans that "while we were still sinners, Christ died for us" (5:8). Jesus died because I was a sinner, not because I was good enough.

For so long I'd been trying to be outwardly good enough – obeying my parents, listening to my teachers, avoiding alcohol abuse, not seeking sexual relations before marriage ... but the burden was huge, and I kept finding my inner desires wanted to rebel. I couldn't keep the act up. And then that day, I realised that God's love for me didn't change depending on how obedient I was. In fact, it had nothing to do with my obedience at all. I realised the full measure of God's love was available to me because Jesus was obedient for me. I realised that I was made good enough through his death. I simply had to invite him to love me.

It's been 10 years since then, and I know I'm different. I'm less scared of what people think. I'm no longer trying to win worth. Before, whenever I was in a social situation, I'd stay quiet, worried about what others would think. But now I look for opportunities to share because it shows what God is like. And even when life is hard, I know that my identity isn't tied up in how well I play soccer, or how many friends I have, or how well I'm doing. I know that there's lasting contentment and value in being accepted as God's son.'

Isn't that wonderful? Corey's new friend at high school joined their tight group of sporty guys. They naturally had things in common. The friend also shared openly with him about being a Christian and invited Corey to go to church 20 times, which is persistent! Corey went along the first time mainly to shut him up, but God was at work. I also love that when Corey arrived at church, he was greeted by lots of people and felt loved for who he was rather than for what he did. I wonder, hypothetically, whether Corey would have been so open to the gospel message if he hadn't sensed that degree of welcome on arrival. We won't know of course, but it's important to keep in mind in our current churches. Are we part of Christian gatherings where visitors feel loved and accepted on arrival? Of course, there are also people among us who may find that degree of attention overwhelming and would rather hide. But most of us need a friendly face or two and a genuine welcome.

After listening to more than 300 faith stories, I think that Corey's description of his journey and underlying thought processes is very common. Even people who have sat in Christian churches all their lives and heard the gospel repeatedly as children and young people may still have a sneaking suspicion that they have to try hard and be good enough. If we could earn God's favour, we think, we might go to heaven. But the tricky thing is, we can never obey all the rules. We cannot please God. We cannot be good enough, which is exactly why Jesus came. He was good enough. He was obedient for us, and his death on the cross made us right with God. We simply have to say yes. May that be the case for all of us today, especially in the moments when we're tempted to revert back to our old 'tick the box' way of thinking instead of accepting God's abundant grace. *Lord, we thank you that we can simply invite you to love us. And then, of course, you reply that, in truth, you already have.*

§

The nature of friendship is, by definition, mutual and generous. We are all drawn to people whom we find trustworthy, honest and likeable. We usually have things in common. This means that if a new friend arrives in our area and invites us to church, even 20 times, our response to them will still be conditional on whether we like them or not. Persistence on its own is not enough. We are all drawn to people we want to hang out with, and we subconsciously decide whether we trust their judgement. Linked to that is our potential attitude towards their professed faith. Would we respect it?

It's interesting to me that in all the faith stories I heard, every person described their friends and key contacts as being trustworthy and likeable. It may seem obvious, but if there is no underlying regard or respect, it's very unlikely that we will respond positively to those kinds of conversations or invitations. That's something to think about! I'd love you to meet **Jodi**, and in particular, notice the way she talked about her new flatmates.

> 'When I was 11, our mother died. It was sudden and unexpected. I'm the eldest of four, with a significantly disabled younger sister and two younger brothers. Afterwards, I carried a lot of hurt. As a people-pleaser, I wanted to fix things for our family in any way I could. Dad was raising us on his own, but I wanted to make things better for everyone. I wanted to fill the gap.
>
> Back then, we used to go to Catholic church on Sundays, as long as there was nothing more important on … like pony club, or horses to ride, or hockey, or soccer. I remember feeling a real arrogance about being Catholic. I had a sense that we had it right and everyone else had it wrong. The priest was between us and God, and he told us how to relate to God. We listened to him on Sundays, but it didn't matter what we did the rest of the week.
>
> After school, I went to university in Albury, country New South Wales, and I had to find my own accommodation. I stumbled

across a Presbyterian church that rented out their manse to students. It was directly across from the uni bar, so I applied! In the application, you had to say you were a Christian, and I lied. I didn't think there were any real Christians anymore!

But when I got there, it took me about three weeks to realise that three of the students were actually Christians. It knocked me over. There was one girl who was kind and friendly. Our rooms were next door to each other, and I liked her! She would pray to God and read her Bible. She spoke about God as if he was someone she knew quite well and who was a significant part of her life. I was really intrigued by that.

She was also relentless, not in a pushy way, but she kept inviting me to campus Bible study. Eventually I went with her. They were a lovely, welcoming group of people. They were reading the Gospel of John together, and they were up to chapter 3. I listened to it, and I thought, 'Wow, this is not the Jesus I knew!' It turned out that God sent Jesus to die for us, to make us right with him, not the other way around.

I'd spent my life trying to do the right things, fixing things for people. But it was God who went to great lengths to make me right with him. That's the God who loves me! It was a slow process, but by the end of the year, I decided I wanted to know God like they did. I wanted a relationship with him like they had. I had been arrogant in my thinking. I'd been carrying hurt and trying to fix everything myself.

I remember the first time I read Romans 8:1. It really resonated with me. We stand before God, holy and pure and blameless, because of what Jesus has done for us. We are not

> condemned. There is nothing his death cannot cover! We can't fix it ourselves, but he can.
>
> Twenty years later, my people-pleasing, fixing-things traits are still there, but God keeps tapping me on the shoulder, gently and regularly, reminding me that he's the one who fixes things and I need to rely on him. I can be a support to people, but I can't put them back together. God is the one who does that ... and I can continue to support and listen and pray.'

Isn't that lovely? Firstly, Jodi noticed that her new neighbour at the university accommodation was kind and friendly. She liked her. At the same time, Jodi was intrigued by the way her neighbour prayed and spoke about God as a real friend. Eventually, when Jodi went with her to campus Bible study and read John 3, she understood God's love. It was that same relationship with God that she wanted – the relationship that she had seen in her friend.

I find Jodi's description of her faith-filled friend both an encouragement and a challenge. It reminds me that this is how God often works, through genuine friendship, even when the friend may be completely unaware of it. But it also challenges me to consider whether I am that kind of open-hearted person, expressing the depth of my relationship with Jesus in vulnerable ways, even with friends who don't currently share my wonder and delight. Do I let the truth of God's presence and grace bubble over in my conversations without unnecessarily editing it out? Do I keep expecting God to work in that way, even after decades of following Jesus? We each need to pray: *Lord, please keep doing your good work in us, that our delight in you would seep out in our conversations today, when it's needed.*

§

There's another aspect of friendship that was consistently described to me in the faith stories. Many people said that knowing their friends were praying for them was a key part of their coming to faith in Jesus. Sometimes, the praying friends were far away in another country. At other times, they were nearby and had gathered to pray for the individual. **Edgar**'s story is a lovely example of this. In his case, the praying friend was his older brother in Mexico.

> 'I became a Christian when I was at university in Mexico. At the time, I was studying mechatronics engineering, and I was living with my older brother in a shared house in Ciudad del Carmen. It was a good time. We were partying and hanging out with friends, like uni students do.
>
> Then, my older brother actually became a Christian. It was a really sudden change in him. He started reading the Bible, listening to sermons and going to church. It really intrigued me.
>
> Before that, I hadn't been thinking about religion. I had no questions about life or faith, nothing. I didn't ever think about it. Then, my brother invited me to his church a couple of times. I went with him, and I heard the gospel. I heard about Jesus. But I didn't understand it. I told my brother I didn't get it. But he was persistent. He kept inviting me to church. I kept telling him that I wasn't interested, and that I wasn't getting anything out of it. It was as if my eyes were closed. That went on for months.
>
> Anyway, one day, we were alone at home. My brother approached me with almost tears in his eyes. He looked very

troubled. He said, "Edgar, I really need you to listen to me." He wanted to tell me about Jesus again.

I said, "But I just don't get it. I don't feel what you feel. I don't see what you see."

Then he said, "Just let me pray for you."

I said, "Okay, you can pray for me."

My brother laid his hand on my shoulder, and he prayed for me. As he prayed, it was like a switch turned on. I felt a warm feeling in my heart. I had this awareness of God, of the Lord Jesus. From that day on, I was able to feel what my brother was feeling. I could see what he could see. We began to go to church together. We read the Bible together. There was a hunger in me to learn more about Jesus. I had that hunger so vividly from that time on. I was 23.

Three years later, I came to Australia, and eventually I went to Bible college to go deeper in the Bible. I even got a scholarship! I was able to get my Bachelor of Theology. At college I also met my wife, who was from Kenya. We got married ... and our plan is to go back to Mexico with a mission agency.

But I have to tell you one more thing. It happened on Sunday. My younger brother (in Mexico) has always been uninterested in Christianity. My older brother and I have been praying for him for eight years now. It has been a really long time of praying. But just last week, my younger brother actually went to church with my older brother, for the first time! It made me feel very encouraged. I know it's hard to pray for family members for a long time. But we can keep praying, like it says

> in 1 John 5:14: "... if we ask anything according to his will, he hears us." And God will make his love and gospel shine, in the right time.'

It's true, as Edgar says, that it can be very hard to pray for friends and family members over long periods. We become tired and perhaps impatient. When and how will we see God at work? It's been decades! For me, hearing stories like Edgar's reminds me not to give up. God is sovereign and utterly good. He will make his love and gospel shine at the right time, as Edgar says. And we continue to pray. In Edgar's case, it's wonderful that the moment of truth occurred for him exactly as his older brother was beside him, hand on his shoulder, praying for him out loud. Imagine the delight in his older brother's heart when he realised what had happened!

I've actually listened to quite a few faith stories where the person described their moment of coming to faith as being the same moment that someone was praying for them in person. Prayer is magnificent and powerful! It is an incredible privilege to come before our holy God in worship and intercession. God hears us always, even when we aren't expecting it. He teaches us and humbles us. He works out his purposes in our lives, even in our weariness.

Did you also notice that in Edgar's case, he didn't describe any outer unravelling? He said he was fine and having a good time. He didn't have any questions about life or faith. He had no outer needs or struggles. But then Edgar's brother became a Christian, and Edgar noticed the change in him. He was intrigued by that change, so he went to church, but he still didn't get it. That went on for months until the day Edgar agreed to prayer, and the switch turned on, and he sensed the reality of Jesus.

That's another thing I've noticed repeatedly when gathering these faith stories. Often, when an unbelieving person sees a close friend or family member become a Christian, then there can be a ripple effect on the people nearby who notice significant outer life changes, which is wonderful. *Lord, we come to you today and we pray for those ripple effects in our neighbourhoods and streets, and in schools and communities across the world. May those ripples be beautifully visible, and may many people be drawn to the Lord Jesus in response.*

§

I'd love to share one more example of the life-changing impact of prayerful support and friendship. In Edgar's case, the support came from his brother, who Edgar knew very well and respected. In contrast, **Badawi** told me he received support and prayer from a person he hardly knew – his university lecturer. In Badawi's case, it made the support all the more striking and compelling.

> 'Growing up in Palestine, with an Islamic background, I knew a few Christians (and what they believed), but I thought they got it wrong.
>
> The first time I knew there was a different story (to the Islamic story) was from a TV cartoon. The cartoon was made in the United States and broadcast from a channel in Cyprus. We would get a weak signal where I lived in Palestine. I remember the cartoon told the stories of the Old and New Testaments. The cartoon was well done for the 80s … and it was fascinating. It made me realise there was a different book and a different faith than Islam.

After that, I clearly remember a radio station in Arabic. It was always on after the 10:20 pm news. It talked about the teachings of Jesus. I used to listen to it as a teenager. I didn't think it was the right way; it was just interesting.

Then I went to university and worked in the medical field. I was mixing with people with wealth and power. That's when Islam stopped making sense to me. I saw a schism between Islamic teaching and behaviour. If Islam is the solution to people's problems, then why don't they live like it? I started to move away from it. It was Ramadan, but I was not fasting. At the same time, there was an ultra-conservative Muslim movement emerging in Palestine, and I thought about leaving the country.

I came to Australia in 2007. I knew nothing about Australia, except for a weird TV show called *Neighbours*. My degree meant nothing here, so I started a master's degree. At the same time, my brother back in Palestine was having medical issues. He was born with congenital problems, and he was back in hospital. I couldn't see him. I felt very stressed. I told my lecturer at the university. He said, "Would you like me to pray for you and your brother?"

It seemed amazing to me. I had started a whole new life 15,000 kilometres away. Nobody knew me here, and I was in a secular country where nobody cared what anyone believed. And yet, the first person I spoke to – someone in a very high position – offered to pray for me and my brother. I said yes.

Afterwards, I wanted to know more about Christianity. I had noticed a Bible college near where I lived. I thought that I couldn't approach a new faith system without studying it, so I went in and asked if I could enrol in a short course.

The person at the Bible college seemed surprised! He said that normally people who studied there were practising believers. Some of them were on the path to ordination. I said, "That's okay, I was just interested." He enrolled me in two subjects: an introduction to the Old Testament and an introduction to the New Testament.

In the first two weeks of being a student at that college, I saw how the students treated me and each other. I saw how they behaved. They lived what they preached. There was no schism. So, I went back to my Christian lecturer at university, and I said, "I want to follow this faith."

That's when I prayed with him, and I became a believer in Jesus. Less than a year later, I was baptised. I found a church where they met in a housing estate and cared for refugees. I went on and did my Master of Theology.

Now, I want to say to people ... listen to the voice that keeps calling you. I was lucky. God didn't leave me. He didn't quit on me, even when I moved 15,000 kilometres away. He put people in my life. And when you accept Jesus into your life, the change will come naturally. It comes from inside you. God helps you. There is a verse in Matthew 11 where Jesus says. "Come to me, all you who are weary and burdened, and I will give you rest" (v. 28). In my Arabic Bible, the verse says, "I will give you comfort". Jesus will take the heavy burdens and he will give us comfort. That's what God has done for me.'

Badawi's life was changed because his university lecturer, who hardly knew him, asked if he could pray for him. And Badawi said yes. Afterwards, he couldn't stop thinking about it – the unexpectedness of it all – his lecturer deliberately caring for him in a new, foreign country where he was not known. As a result, Badawi went immediately off to enrol in Bible college as an unbeliever, wanting to find out more about Christianity. Imagine being the person at reception that day, obviously surprised by Badawi's request to study the Bible. But then, Badawi began his studies and carefully watched the other students around him, who were naturally kind to him and each other. He saw that there was no schism, and Badawi was persuaded by the gospel, at least in part because his fellow students lived the teachings of Jesus with integrity. This is absolutely wonderful! *Lord, we ask today that you would help us be people who live out our faith in you at home, at work, on the train, wherever we are – in weariness, delight and everything in between – because of your great, consuming love for us.*

§

Of course, there is no limit to the ways our trusted friends point us to the gospel – sometimes it's in their warmth, words, actions, prayers, consistency or lives of radical faith. I could go on and give many examples of this, but in essence, friends pour out their spiritual gifts in front of us, often unknowingly. Meet **Brenda**, who was drawn to faith in Jesus at age 59, partly because her friendly neighbours played beautiful music.

> 'I've just turned 60. Up until a year ago, I didn't pay very much attention to my spiritual life. I was busy, working full-time as a primary school teacher and caring for my mum, who was in a

nursing home with Parkinson's Disease. As a child, I had grown up in a loving family with Christian values, but from my teenage years onwards, I decided I wasn't interested in religion. I wanted to get out there and have fun and play sport!

A year ago, though, everything changed. I live in an amazing complex of townhouses, and I have beautiful neighbours – James and Emma. They go to the local Baptist church, and James is in the church band. I used to hear him practising his music next door and it was beautiful ... so one day, I asked if I could come along on a Sunday to hear him perform.

That was the beginning of it. I walked into their church, and it felt overwhelming. Immediately, the sense of community, fellowship and love hit me! There must have been 300 people there, and the music was so powerful. I'd never heard anything like it! As I watched the congregation sing with such intent and passion, praying with their arms raised, I knew there was something special happening there and I wanted to pursue it further!

I started going, week in, week out. I'd have cups of tea with Emma and James and ask them all my questions. They told me about an Alpha evangelistic course, and I attended that. The first session was drawing on all the facts. I needed to have it confirmed through evidence that the Bible and its contents were not a made-up story but factual. Jesus was a historical human. The Bible was confirmed, within itself, over time and by different authors. It was backed up by the Dead Sea Scrolls. I soaked it all in. After five weeks, I picked up the Bible myself and started reading the Gospels. I couldn't put it down. I was reading until 2 o'clock in the morning! It was all beginning to make sense to me!

Then we discussed the Holy Spirit. The leader encouraged us all to close our eyes and say, "Holy Spirit, come." Nothing happened at first, but then I went home and couldn't sleep, so I sat on my bed and kept repeating, "Holy Spirit, come." I suddenly felt this incredible wave move through my body, from the top of my head to the tips of my toes. I knew that the Holy Spirit had found me.

That was in July last year! I was baptised in January this year. I've been learning so much about Jesus. In March, I went on a historical tour to Israel with John Dickson and others. It was incredible to be in the land that Jesus once lived in. I now read the Bible and the text comes alive. I can visualise all the places!

Two weeks after I returned from Israel, though, I had a routine check-up and they found cancer in both of my breasts. I was suddenly facing a double mastectomy and reconstruction surgery. But I was blown away by the fact that I was now a Christian and I had the power of prayer. I had so many people praying for me and supporting me through the journey. It was massive, but I had a sense that God was by my side. He wouldn't leave me.

I remember early on, being struck by Matthew 7:7–8, "Ask and it will be given to you; seek and you will find; knock and the door will be opened to you." I now take time each day to pray and learn more of the wisdom of God. I feel so grateful to have found God!'

Again, it's a wonderful testimony. Like Edgar, Brenda didn't specifically describe any unravelling in her life, although she was very busy caring for her mother and working full-time as a teacher. It all changed in a moment, though, when she heard her neighbour James playing beautiful music and she wanted to hear more of it. She visited their church for that purpose and was overwhelmed by the sense of community and love. She watched the congregation singing with passion and was intrigued.

This is such a powerful reminder. Genuine worship of our gracious God is a witness. Worship music can draw people into truth. Beautiful practice music can float next door to a listening neighbour, and God is at work in it all. I also love the description of Brenda needing answers to her historicity questions. She read the Bible and couldn't put it down. She prayed for the Holy Spirit and she was absolutely convinced of the Spirit's presence. It's such a lovely mix in this story, with all the beautiful ingredients – neighbours, music, worship, church, the word, the message, evidence and the Holy Spirit. Sometimes, I think I'm tempted to unpick the stories too much, trying to find the core ingredient. But they are often all there, pointing to the wonderful, life-giving answers in Jesus. May more and more people find those answers this year in our towns and cities.

§

As humans, we are often very immediate creatures. We are present in this moment, today, with the people around us. Even when we pray, we prefer to see immediate answers from God. If we don't, we assume that God is busy somewhere else or perhaps unconcerned with us. But the wonderful truth is that God exists outside of time in ways we can't even fathom. He is at work right now, today, and also in the years to come. We may never fully understand it, but our failure to comprehend God's immortality and timelessness doesn't preclude it. Meet **Louise**, who described the impact of a neighbour on her faith. In this case, though, she said it was an old *memory* of her neighbour's faith that changed her life.

> 'I grew up in a housing commission place in western Sydney. It was pretty rough. My dad worked night shifts, so we didn't see him very much, but we were all close to my mother.
>
> After school, I started a degree in literature, which I enjoyed very much. But at the beginning of my second year, I was visiting a friend and I got a call from a paramedic. He said my mother had died. It was sudden and horrific. She'd had an asthma attack at home. My father, younger brother and sister were there when it happened. They tried to revive her before the ambulance came. They watched her pass away.
>
> It was an incredibly difficult time. I quit my uni degree. We couldn't even pay for my mum's funeral. I got a full-time job, and I became responsible for everything in the home – cooking, cleaning, shopping, paying bills, supervising homework, and driving my younger brother and sister around.
>
> I was barely an adult myself, only 19. My dad wasn't coping at all. He would come home from work and stare at the walls. There was nobody to talk to. My friends at the time didn't understand the load I was carrying. So, I learnt to hold it in and keep going.

After 12 months I was in a really bad place. I remember waking up and thinking, "If God isn't real, I'm not sure there's any purpose to this, or any hope at all."

Some years earlier, we'd had Christian neighbours. Our house was semidetached and there was a small brick fence out the front. Our neighbours would often be out the front when we were coming in or going out. Their mum would deliberately connect with us and share her faith in Jesus. She even took us to her church a couple of times. But they moved out just after Mum died, and I didn't know where they were. I wanted to talk to her, but I had no way of getting in contact.

So, I decided to give her old church a call. I explained over the phone that my mum had died, and I was very depressed. I said, "I think I need Jesus."

The person on the phone said, "Come down here right now." So I did. I met with a youth leader, who was fantastic. She sat me down and listened to me. I was able to talk for the first time. Within a few weeks, I decided to become a Christian. It was mostly because I realised that God was there in the midst of it. He had a plan and a purpose, even when it didn't feel like it. God was at work through everything.

I went home and told my family. I said the gospel made sense to me. I said that my faith in Jesus had made a big difference to me, and I encouraged them to come to church. My dad became a Christian within the year. It wasn't magical or overnight, but things definitely changed for us. Life was still hard, but there was meaning and purpose. My dad became a changed person, after being quite angry and aggressive before.

> To me, it speaks about fruitfulness. Our neighbours witnessed to us for years, and they didn't see any fruit. But when it became crunch time for me, I called the church. It reminds me that we're called to sow the seeds, or water the seeds, and God brings the fruit, like it says in 1 Corinthians 3:6: "I [Paul] planted the seed, Apollos watered it, but God has been making it grow." I want to say to people, if you're sharing Jesus with your neighbours, or the people you love, and it doesn't feel like you're getting anywhere, don't give up.
>
> Amazingly, just last year, our neighbour made contact with me again, 25 years later. I told her what had happened – that I'd come to faith in Jesus, and that now I have three theological degrees and I lecture at Bible college. I told her that she'd been part of my story. She was amazed.
>
> But it's the same for all of us. We never know when our words will make a difference for someone … maybe God will use them today.'

This is a wonderfully important story, reminding us that God works in his timing, over decades, often using tiny seeds. Louise's neighbours sowed all those tiny seeds over a red brick fence, and it wasn't until many years later, when Louise was at her rock bottom, that she remembered them. The Spirit worked in her heart and caused Louise to reach out to the church. The Spirit also worked through the words of the person on the phone, as well as the youth leader at church, who listened to her and loved her. Louise responded to the gospel and came to faith in Jesus. God brings the fruit!

I especially love the postscript. Imagine how the neighbour must have felt, 25 years later, when she found out what had happened!

It also makes me realise that there must be so many stories like Louise's, where the 'sowers' of the tiny seeds never find out what happened on this earth. They don't get the phone call or the email decades later. Perhaps that's you and me. Maybe today we can keep offering those tiny seeds to God, not knowing what will happen but trusting that God will bring about growth in his good timing.

§

There's another trend in these stories that I find compelling. Almost everyone I spoke to mentioned, at some point in their journey, the experience of visiting a church or a gathering of believers. Some years ago, I remember talking to a young man who came to faith in Jesus in China. He had been struggling with extreme parental expectations and feelings of hopelessness. One day, he said he went to the top of a tall building with the idea of throwing himself out the window. But as he leaned out the window, he saw a church below him. He could see that the people were welcoming and happy. He wanted to know why. So, he left the building and went downstairs to investigate. His story continues today, and he's had his ups and downs since then, but the simple fact is that seeing those smiling people in the church saved his life that day. And the church across the world, in all its different guises, continues to be the place where God works to grow his people in knowledge, faith and fellowship in Jesus.

We all know that there are major struggles within the church. There always have been, and there always will be. We know that in many Western churches, numbers are declining. Conflict, power plays and moral failures have had disastrous effects. Humans often bring out the worst in each other. But miraculously, God continues to work through his body in the church around the world. He is still bringing about his good purposes through frail humans and imperfect church gatherings. Despite it all, people like Louise, Brenda, Tim, Corey and thousands of others are coming to faith in Jesus around Australia through the witness of gathered believers in churches! And local churches are continuing to be safe places for the neediest people in our society. Here's **Melissa**'s story.

> 'I grew up in a loving home and I had a great childhood, full of friends and hobbies. But when I was in Year 7, I started to get bullied pretty badly at school, which turned into self-harm. By the time I was 15, I was drinking and smoking pot. One night I was at a party, and I was raped. I didn't tell anyone, as I blamed myself. I used substances to deal with it.
>
> I dropped out of school at 17 and met a guy who introduced me to speed and ecstasy. We used it occasionally. When I was 18, my best friend died in a car accident. It was really hard. Not long after he passed, I fell pregnant. I stopped drinking for a while, and I had a little boy. But after he was born, I fell in with a different crowd and they introduced me to ice. Then I got into a relationship that spiralled into domestic violence. My using of ice increased to deal with the pain.
>
> We were often being raided by the police and arrested on drug charges. At that time, I gave my son to my parents because I couldn't keep him safe. I continued on the path to self-destruction, as a means to take away the pain. It numbed my feelings of self-hate, blame and depression.

In my mid-20s, I ended up getting charged with drug trafficking. I had to go to prison for a short period. After I got out, I kept using ice and selling drugs ... and I went back in. It happened a few times in 2016. The last time I got arrested, it was a few days before my son's birthday. They wouldn't let me see him. I'd never missed his birthday before. It was my rock bottom. I couldn't see him on the one day that mattered most.

I tried to hang myself in the watch house. I thought that everyone would be better off without me. But I was found and taken to hospital, where they referred me to a drug rehab program run by the Salvation Army. I arrived there in December 2016, completely broken.

The Salvation Army loved me back to life. During my time there, I realised that something had to change. My child needed me. I started going to a Salvation Army church and I did the Alpha course. It really opened my heart to a loving, powerful God. I knew he was present in my life. He'd already done such wonderful things in keeping me alive.

Part-way through my time in rehab, I had to go to the Supreme Court for my drug charges. I was seven months clean by then. But I knew I was looking at a four-year sentence. It was pretty intense, knowing it was my last day of freedom. But at the end of the hearing, my barrister unexpectedly asked for a shortened sentence and immediate parole. The judge agreed. He could see I was trying to live a better life and that I was no threat to society.

> It was the beginning of my whole new life! It was magical. The church people really cared for me, and the more I went to church, the more I built relationships. Without their support, I never would have stayed clean. They saved my life.
>
> I began to pray every day. My faith in God filled the void that had ruled my existence. I came to see that God really does save us, even those of us whom society deems unworthy.
>
> Now I'm working in a drug rehab place myself. I'm a support worker helping other addicts on their recovery journey. I want to say that it's always possible to recover when you have love and support!
>
> My favourite verse is from Jeremiah 29:11. "'For I know the plans I have for you,' declares the Lord, 'plans to prosper you and not to harm you, plans to give you a hope and a future.'" Reading that truth always warms my heart. I know that I'm not walking this path alone. Jesus is with me. And even if my plans don't work out the way I want, I know that God's plans are always good.'

In Melissa's case, the church literally loved her back to life. They became her family. They cared for her, without reservation. They were the feet and hands of Jesus. Without them, Melissa said she would never have stayed clean. Praise God for gatherings like that. In very similar ways to Scott, Mike, Kaz, Tim and so many others, Melissa found hope, healing and the truth of God's love through her local church community.

It goes without saying that for anyone reading this who is in similar depths of despair, please reach out and seek help. There are multiple organisations available who provide free, 24-hour help.* You are not alone. As well as that, there may be people in a nearby church who would love to be available for you today, to pray for you and listen to you. They may also be able to refer you to an appropriate external organisation. And for all of us who are part of church gatherings, may we continue to represent Jesus to a watching, needy, fractured society full of people like Melissa. May we all move away from staid preconceptions of groups of 'moralising geriatrics' (as Mike expected) and become the people of God who love and serve Jesus, and love and serve the people in our communities unreservedly, in all our different styles and forms. I thank God for Melissa's testimony and indeed for all those who have been drawn to Jesus through imperfect humans just like us, and through imperfect human gatherings just like ours. As the writer of Hebrews says, '… let us consider how we may spur one another on towards love and good deeds, not giving up meeting together, as some are in the habit of doing, but encouraging one another – and all the more as you see the Day approaching' (10:24–25). May God continue to use our gatherings in surprising and miraculous ways as he draws more and more people into his family.

---

* For example, the Lifeline hotline 13 11 14. Lifeline is a national charity providing all Australians experiencing emotional distress with access to 24-hour crisis support and suicide prevention services (lifeline.org.au).

4
Bible truths

In the stories I collected, one clear trend emerged that may seem ridiculously obvious, but I'm glad it's there. Every person who talked to me about coming to faith in Jesus also told me about the first time they read the Bible. They didn't always read the Bible immediately, though. Many of my friends in Nepal, for example, came to faith in Jesus out of Hinduism, and they didn't have immediate access to a Bible. They were not always literate. Many of them only read the Bible in the years afterwards, once they had access to it or their literacy changed. However, in Australia, the majority of people I spoke to had access to a Bible, and they read it early on.

Perhaps it might be good to pause here and reflect on our own faith journeys. Do you remember the first time you read any portion of the Bible by yourself? Where did you start? What was your response back then? As I mentioned earlier, I remember pouring through my paperback Good News New Testament, tucked up in my bed at age 12. I started at the Gospel of Matthew, and I was immediately drawn to the person of Jesus – his words, his welcome, his healing touch and his challenge to the crowds. But it was many years after that that I got my hands on an Old Testament and attempted to read the whole thing. It was even more years after that before I understood the sweep of the Bible – that Jesus was, in fact, the answer to every unspoken longing since the beginning of time.

4. Bible truths

We know that the Bible is God's word to us in written form, but it is also a complex, ancient text, with multiple styles and authors, and it can be hard to read. I remember the first time I read it through from beginning to end; I was struck by the huge, overarching narrative. More than anything, I realised the Bible describes *God's* story and world. Everything we see and hear belongs to God. He is the centre and the reason. He formed all things out of nothing. He made order and beauty out of chaos. He made humankind in his own image – the pinnacle of his creative work – for the *purpose* of relationship with him and with each other. It's incredible and breathtaking. But of course, in reading further, it didn't last. God gave his people a choice, and the people chose something different and distorted – their own food, their own way, their own answers. And everything that was good at the start became tarnished. It's such a heavy beginning. That choice (that was not so distant from us) produced pain and toil, evil alongside good, ugliness alongside beauty, and dying alongside life. The people were driven away from the glorious presence of God.

But in all of that awfulness, as we read the Bible, we also realise that the narrative sets up one all-consuming question. What will God do to restore his world and his people? What will he do to bring his people home? Will there be beauty and flourishing again? Will evil ever be defeated?

I remember the first time I read through Genesis, I was amazed at God's good plan. He said he would bring hope and blessing to the nations through Abraham's family, as revealed in chapter 12. Yet reading further, the narrative also felt slow to me, and even horrifying. The text moved so quickly from beauty and generosity to disobedience, envy, murder and every kind of evil. I could see God's mercy and patience, but I could also see human disobedience and forgetfulness in all its colours. I had so many questions. How would God, who is holy and righteous, resolve this? Would he override his promises, or would he overlook the sins of the people? The spiral seemed to worsen in Judges, 1 and 2 Samuel, 1 and 2 Kings, and 1 and 2 Chronicles, to the point that I found it difficult to read. God seemed to keep making promises, including to David – that he would give him a descendant who would rule forever – but when? There were also glimpses of obedience and faithfulness, miracles and wonder, but it was set in a context of exile, hardship, lament and silence.

Until, *finally*, 1,000 years after that promise, God did the impossible. He came himself, incarnate, the Lord Jesus Christ, as a baby in Mary's womb. He came to redeem and restore and bring hope. And as Jesus began his ministry, the crowds flocked to him. It was his upside-down grace and mercy as he taught and healed and spoke to those who didn't belong. He offered them hope and forgiveness. And of course, many of the people believed.

But not everyone. On a Thursday evening, Jesus was arrested in the garden, taken to the authorities and crucified. He let the nails pierce his own hands, and he let the breath escape from his own lungs. The crowd sneered at him. But Jesus, the Son of God, forgave them. And then he died, and the sun disappeared. The people wept – all of their hopes finished and buried in an unused tomb.

Except, it wasn't over. Somehow, the worst kind of suffering was part of God's plan. God stayed true to his holiness as well as his grace. In the cross of Christ, God absorbed the curse of sin into himself. That's how much he loved the world. He didn't override his promises or overlook the sin of the people. And three days later, Jesus rose from the dead. The tomb was found empty, and everything changed from that moment for the world. Sin and death were defeated forever, for all time, for us.

And we are invited into the story. I love the book of Acts. When God sent his Holy Spirit, the witness was immediate. Three thousand people responded. There were healings, awe and wonder, as well as persecution and trials. Incredibly, within it all, the news of the risen Lord Jesus spread to the entire ancient world. And then it spread to us, in the centuries since, in our tiny pockets of the world, oceans and continents away from Jerusalem, so that we might also respond to the good news, as revealed to us in God's word, the Bible.

It's amazing! Through the Bible, God speaks to each of us personally and intimately. We find ourselves in its pages. We understand the grace of Jesus because we have sat with the terrible weight of the problem within ourselves and within the history of the world. But engaging with the Bible can also be a long journey. My own decades of reading the Bible have reminded me that the process of engaging with Scripture can be very long. There are many parts of it that still seem unfathomable to me. We continue to wrestle with the text and grow in understanding over our entire lives. We are also impacted by the types of Bible teaching and exposition we receive. But in the midst of it all, God speaks powerfully through his word! Meet **Ray**, who told me that he bargained with God. He agreed that he would read the Bible, but only if God would convince him of its truth, quickly.

> 'I grew up in a devout Maltese Australian Roman Catholic home, which meant we went to Mass three times a week. To be

Maltese was to be Catholic. No matter how tired my parents were at the end of the week, we always went to Mass.

I have lots of fond memories of my upbringing. My mother taught me that God was personal, and it left a lasting and profound impression on me. Our parish priest was deeply loved by everyone in the community, and I remember him patiently answering my questions like, "Can a child be a pope?" I clearly remember learning the doctrine of the Trinity from my Filipino nun in second class. There is one God, who is made up of three persons: Father, Son and Spirit. I feel indebted to the foundation I received.

Nevertheless, as I grew older, it became clear that whatever relationship I claimed to have with God, it was very much on my terms. It was amazing what lifestyle choices I got him to agree with. He had become a god of my imagination.

After school, I went to university and met a friend who came from a home that didn't believe in God. To my surprise, she suddenly became passionate about Jesus. It didn't take me long to realise that she had something I didn't have. The living Jesus was very real in her life. One day, she challenged me. She said that Jesus was either Lord of everything, or he was a liar or a lunatic. She said I needed to make a decision. Who did I think he was? I could see her logic, but I didn't want to think about the implications of Jesus being Lord of my life. By that stage I was in party mode and living in Bondi, Sydney. I put the idea on the backburner and tried not to think about it.

Sometime later, I was counselling an alcoholic woman at a rehabilitation centre as part of my social-work training. It was then that I realised I had no reason to care for others. Not even my loving family background could give me a reason to put others before myself. It was a kind of an existential crisis. I dropped out of social work and fell into a series of dead-end casual jobs. Then one morning, while working around Dover Heights, it came into my mind that if Christianity was true and Jesus was really the Son of God, then I was probably in big trouble.

At the same time, I remembered a promise of Jesus. "Ask and it will be given to you; seek and you will find" (Matt 7:7). So, I made a pact with God. I promised to read the Bible, and I asked him to persuade me within three weeks if it was true. Patience was never one of my virtues!

I started reading the Gospels, trying to find out if Jesus was the eternal Son of God. It was the first time I'd truly read the Bible with an open mind, as an adult, and it was a profound experience. I knew a lot of the stories, but what was completely new was the portrait of Jesus that emerged. I simply fell in love with him. There was a ring of truth about everything Jesus said and did. This was the Son of God, in all his glory, and I couldn't deny it.

Several weeks later, I was in Hotel Bondi with two of my friends. They knew I'd been reading the Bible and were concerned for me. As a result, they tried to dissuade me from becoming a Christian by telling me all the things I'd have to change in my life. Since we sinned in similar ways, they could be very

> specific! As they spoke, I imagined a fork in the road of my life. I could keep living on my own terms, doing all those things for the next 60 years, and be cut off from God forever. Or I could surrender to Jesus as Lord, make a completely fresh start, and enjoy forgiveness now and acceptance on the last day. I said, "Guys, I think you've just persuaded me. I'm a Christian!"
>
> They thought, at the time, that it was a phase I was going through. It's now been 41 years. I can't begin to tell you the joy that came into my life. It was as if my whole life I was freefalling until I landed on the truth and love of the Lord Jesus.'

Praise God for the way he worked in Ray's life! Ray made a pact with God, promising to read the Bible if God could persuade him of its truth within three weeks. And he was persuaded! Not only was Ray convinced of the truth of the Bible, but he was also personally convicted of his own need for Jesus. If Jesus was the eternal Son of God, then Ray needed to make a response and surrender to him as Lord.

I think Ray's story is an excellent reminder to all of us that if the Bible is true, then it makes serious claims on our lives. We cannot simply read the Bible as a historical 'novel' or an interesting account of the origins of life. If God is God, then we are his created people. We are in a different position before him. We need to respond to Jesus as Lord, as Ray did.

I love the way that Ray described that particular decision. As he sat with his mates at Bondi, he knew that he could either continue on the same path for another 60 years or make a fresh start and enjoy forgiveness now and acceptance on the last day. Forty-one years later,

Ray is so thankful. He can't describe the joy that has come into his life since that surrender.

This reminds me that surrendering to Jesus is not just about avoiding alienation from God at the end of our lives. It means walking with Jesus right now, and as we do, we are given wisdom, joy and much-needed hope today! *Lord, we thank you for the joy you give us in knowing you, every day. Thank you that it is beyond description!*

§

Most often, when people read the Bible for the first time in Australia, they come to it with at least a small amount of information. They know that the Bible is a Christian book, and their minds approach it in a certain way as a result. Interestingly, some years ago, I met **Yvonne** through a mutual friend. She told me that when she first read the Bible in China, she had no idea what she was actually reading.

> 'I was born in the 1970s in mainland China. I was lucky. It was before the one-child policy, so I had siblings. My father was a businessperson, driven by creating wealth. It was his security. He had a very poor background, so he was diligent in making money. But it was also the time of the communist party, so making wealth was illegal. The communist philosophy is that everyone should be equal. One year, my father was taken to gaol for operating a business. It added to the insecurity we all felt. Then, in 1990, China opened up and the economy changed. That's when I became part of the family business, intent on establishing my own kingdom. It was the most important thing – security. I had to rely on myself.

At the same time, my parents practised ancestor worship. They wanted fortune and good luck, so they often went to the temple to pray for prosperity. But I wasn't keen on religion. I thought that Buddhism was for the fool and Christianity for the weak. I also assumed that Christianity was for Westerners, and I wasn't interested in it.

When I was 25, I moved out of home. One day, I went to the library to find something to read. I found a book with a black cover, titled *Old Testament* and *New Testament*. I had never heard of it, so I opened the book and started reading. I read a story about Jacob wrestling with God. I thought it was Greek mythology, so I borrowed it. In China, you pay money per day to borrow a book from the library, and you put down a deposit.

I went home and I read the book as a novel. I didn't understand much of it, but I liked the stories and the wisdom literature. The Psalms touched my heart. At the end of the month, I hadn't finished reading the book, but I had to return it to the library. I was tempted to keep it. I knew I had to pay more money, but when I got to the library, the boss said, "You've been reading the Bible! I shouldn't charge you to read the Bible."

He gave me my money back. I was so surprised. I didn't know I was reading the Bible!

I said, "I haven't finished reading it. Where can I buy a copy?"

He said, "You should go to the local church. They will have a Bible."

The following Sunday, I went to the local Christian church. Someone gave me a hymn book as I went in. I can still

4. Bible truths

remember the words of the first hymn. It was called, "Come Home, Come Home." I sang along, and it felt like a song from heaven. I was crying. It felt like someone was calling me home. I didn't understand much of the sermon, but the prayer was beautiful for me.

When the service finished, I didn't know what to do. The old lady next to me went forward to pray, so I copied her. I listened to her prayers. She was praying for other people. It was so beautiful and urgent. I had never heard a prayer like that. At the Buddhist temple, we only ever prayed for wealth for our own family. So, I said to God, "Wow, if you are real, I want you to be my God."

That was the beginning. I kept going back to church. I purchased a Bible and I read it all. I understood it, step by step, and I started my journey of knowing Christ. Now, 20 years later, I'm a pastor in a Mandarin-speaking church in Sydney. Jesus is so real to me! And his words in the Bible are so precious to me! I want to proclaim his word! Looking back, I didn't know much when I first responded to God. But we don't always have a full concept of God when we respond. I knew I was loved by God. And I've been through many hard times. But God has cared for me. I've had to learn to rely on Jesus, and not on myself. My favourite verse is Isaiah 43:1: "Do not fear, for I have redeemed you; I have summoned you by name; you are mine."'

Yvonne's story is beautiful, showing us again that God is wonderfully personal in the way he reveals himself to us. He knew that Yvonne had preconceived ideas about Christianity, thinking it was for the weak or the Westerner. Possibly, if Yvonne had known she was borrowing a Christian Bible from the library, she would never have taken it home. But she didn't know, which was the lovely part of this story. She took the Bible home, read it as a novel and really liked it, especially the Psalms and wisdom literature. Something inside her wanted to keep reading it, not knowing what it was. Imagine her surprise when she talked to the librarian. I also love the fact that when she went to church, she heard another lady praying, and she really wanted to know a God like that, even though that's all she knew. It was the contrast with the prayers she had heard growing up. And yet again, it's the impact of worship, prayer and God's word. All of Yvonne's story seems so lovely and personal. God was truly summoning her by name, which is, of course, the essence of God's nature, as he reveals himself to each of us.

I also appreciated Yvonne's comment that she didn't know very much when she first responded to God. All she knew was that she was loved by God. And afterwards, she understood truth slowly and gradually, as she read more and more of the Bible and came to know Jesus more and more. It's the same for all of us. *Lord, we thank you that we can begin at the beginning, and that you remain the same, slowly revealing yourself to us in Christ.*

§

Yvonne's story perhaps sounds surprising to many of us because we find it hard to imagine reading the Bible for the first time without knowing what it is. What would we make of it? Would Genesis 32 sound like Greek mythology to us? Would we want to keep reading? I think it's hard to imagine because most of us are familiar with the Bible, having either grown up reading it or in a society where key texts are known and repeated. We at least understand that the Bible is a

Christian book. But the wonderful thing is that no matter how many times we've read it before, God's word to us is alive and active. The Holy Spirit speaks through it, convicting our hearts every day and reminding us of God's holiness and restorative plan. As Paul wrote to Timothy not long before he died: 'All Scripture is God-breathed and is useful for teaching, rebuking, correcting and training in righteousness' (2 Tim 3:16). We agree with Paul that the Bible is God's living word to us. It is good and true and useful in every part of life, for every age. It can even speak to our hearts in a fresh way, many years after we have wandered far away. **Andrew**'s story is a lovely example of that.

> 'My wife and I both grew up in the church in Canberra. We were very involved. My father was the youth director. But after we got married, we slipped away a bit. We moved to Melbourne, and then we bought a farm in Sutton, New South Wales, and then another farm in Cowra. Both farms were 1000 acres, and we were breeding Limousin cattle. I was often away on Sundays, at agricultural shows and on the different properties.
>
> By the time I was 40, we had three kids and we were living on the farm in Cowra. The soil there was very rich and had the potential to grow anything we wanted. We purchased it so we could feed the stock during drought. It was a busy time. When you make lucerne hay, you have to wait for the dew to settle on it. I'd be out there at 10 pm at night, bailing the hay, then up again at 5 am, raking the hay. During the day, I'd be moving the irrigation pipes, sowing things, ploughing things, feeding

the cattle, doing embryo transplants, fencing, running our own butcher shop in town and delivering meat to Sydney.

But it was also beautiful. We had a river on our property, with huge river gums. And stepping out of the tractor after making hay at midnight is magnificent. The stars are so bright they light up the ground. They are so close.

One day, I'd just planted a new crop of oats. There were little green shoots coming up everywhere. I was sitting near the riverbank. It was quiet and beautiful. I started thinking. What's this all about? What's the point of all this busyness and beauty?

I went back inside, and I found an old Bible that had belonged to my dad. I hadn't read it for years. It opened up at Romans 12:2: "Do not conform to the pattern of this world, but be transformed by the renewing of your mind. Then you will be able to test and approve what God's will is – his good, pleasing and perfect will."

It was a major moment for me, a big change in the direction of my life. I realised I needed to let God transform me. That's the only thing that would help me find true purpose. And part of that was being connected at church, so we started going to the local church and to Bible study. It was really good. I started to spend a lot of time praying while I was on the tractor, which was all day. My mind started focusing on kingdom things. I talked a lot to our pastor. We bounced off each other, and my wife and I became involved in ministry.

After a few years, I went to Sydney and trained for the ministry, and then we planted a church in western Sydney. It's been wonderful. I don't have regrets, but it's also been hard. I'm a bit more wary now when I read that verse! I know things can go wrong … but perhaps that's a good thing. Maybe I'm more aware of God's presence and strength. Maybe I'm more aware that he's the one leading things, controlling things, and putting us in the places he needs us to be.

And I still love the beauty of fields and rivers and growing things. But nowadays, whenever I see beauty, it points me to the glory of God.'

I'm sure we've all had moments like Andrew. We've picked up the Bible and been struck to the heart by a fresh truth in a particular verse. But for Andrew, it had been 20 years since he last picked up a Bible. He had become immersed in his life on the land, planting, growing, harvesting and raising their children and animals. He and his wife hadn't been attending church or thinking about God at all. But he still had questions. What is all this beauty about? What is the point of it all?

Perhaps we all carry those questions deep inside us, whether in busyness, beauty or unravelling. Andrew's response to the beauty and the questions inside him was to go and find an old Bible. As he picked it up, the Lord led him to Romans 12, and the words spoke deeply to him, convicting his heart. It's a wonderful passage. Paul was writing to the church in Rome, reminding them that God had shown them abundant mercy in Christ. So, in view of that mercy, they were to offer themselves as a living sacrifice to God and let God transform them.

It's true for all of us. Andrew said that the truth of those verses changed his life in every way. For the very first time, he understood his purpose in Christ. May we each look to God in fresh ways today for the answers to our deepest questions. And may we each let God slowly transform us, renewing our minds, in every small act, both mundane and marvellous.

§

Of course, as well as being God's inspired word to us, the Bible can be challenging to read. It is an ancient text, a collection of 66 books written by at least 40 different authors over a period of 1,500 years. Within it, there are multiple genres and styles, from poetry and history to epistles and wisdom literature. This means that the reader needs to take context and authorship into account, as well as the span of Scripture and the promises of God in Christ. Reading the Bible can take time and courage! But within all of that, God makes himself known, even to a first-time reader. I'd love you to meet **Karen**.

> 'When I was 16, my parents divorced. It was fairly ugly. Immediately afterwards, I had to look after my younger siblings. Then, as my mum started to recover, I became severely depressed.
>
> I decided to fix the black hole in myself by aiming to be top in my year. I studied furiously, and at the end of Year 11, I came top in seven subjects. But as soon as it was announced, the despair rushed back in. It hadn't fixed the black hole. I felt even worse because I'd done everything I could ... and it hadn't worked.
>
> Over the next few months, I tried to work out how to commit suicide and make it look like an accident. I didn't want to upset my mum. Later, in Year 12, I let slip to my mum what I was

thinking, and she freaked out. She said two significant things to me.

Firstly, she said she wanted me to go to church. That was strange, because she didn't go to church herself and we weren't a Christian family.

Secondly, she said, "If you don't have faith in something outside of yourself, when life goes bad, you've got nothing."

She took me to church the next day. The first thing I noticed was the constant "stand up, sit down" repetition. It was bizarre. The sermon was on Hannah. I'd never heard of Hannah. But halfway through the sermon, the minister said, "If you don't have faith in something outside of yourself, when life goes bad, you've got nothing."

Those were his exact words. I nearly died. My first thought was, "Maybe there *is* a God!" My brain went into meltdown. I started to wonder … if there is a God, what do I do about it? I can't just ignore a God!

I went home, scratched around and found a Bible that someone had given us. I read from the beginning – Genesis, Exodus and half of Leviticus. I read every footnote! I thought if I kept reading, then sooner or later, it would make sense to me. It didn't make sense. My only thought was that God was God and I was not.

And … if God was God, then I was sure he wasn't happy with me. I was a vile teenager. I used to lie awake at night and plot how to be hurtful to my friends and brothers. I don't even know how I had any friends.

I also worked out I was completely incapable of fixing the mess inside me, so God had to do it. Weeks later, I went back to church, and afterwards, a bunch of us went out to a pizza restaurant. I remember the others were talking about Jesus. I desperately wanted to know about Jesus, but I refused to ask. I sat at the table, arms folded, leaning back. In the middle of the conversation, a light went on: "Jesus is how God fixes the mess!"

I went home and prayed, "Jesus, I've screwed up my life. You can have it, if you want. Amen."

In that moment, God filled me with joy. I hadn't felt joy or purpose for years. God utterly changed me from the inside out. He saved me spiritually and physically. There was no way I would still be alive today if God hadn't saved me.

At university, I was a different person, radically changed. Jesus was the best news I'd ever heard ... and I couldn't help but tell everyone. In the three years I was at university, nine of my friends became Christians. Later, I became a university student worker. I've been working on campuses for 30 years – in Sydney, Melbourne, Spain, Belgium. I've seen heaps of people come to faith in Jesus.

I realised, though, that there was still mess inside me. I was changed, but I still suffered from depression. The weakness of my depression over the years has meant I constantly recognise God's work in me. I know deeply that God's work doesn't rely on me. He is doing his thing, in his time, for his glory. It's always about his glory, even in my weakness.'

It's another wonderful testimony. Karen read the Bible from the beginning, including every footnote ... and she didn't understand it. She said that by the time she was halfway through Leviticus, she had only absorbed one thing – God was God, and she wasn't. When Karen told me that part of her story, I smiled and said I thought that was a pretty good thing to realise halfway through Leviticus! It's true that God is God, and we are not. It's true that Jesus is the only way to fix the mess inside us, and we need to trust him. It's also true, as Karen says, that even as believers, we can still feel weak. We are not in heaven yet. We still carry pain and scars. But God invites us to come to him. And as Paul says in 2 Corinthians 12, it's in our weakness that God displays his immeasurable strength, over and over again (v. 9). *Lord, we thank you again that you are God, and we are not. We ask you to reveal your wonderful strength to us today, even in our ongoing weakness and questions.*

§

As I've been writing this chapter on the power of God's word in our lives – the sharp-edged sword, the invitation, the truth and the wonderful, personal life-changing revelation – I've been so thankful for God's truth. At the same time, I've received an email from our friends who work in Bible translation across the world. They wrote (this week) that when they began working in this field back in 2001, the estimate of language communities in the world that still required Bible translation was about 3,000. In the following 20 years, that number slowly reduced to 2,000 languages. However, since the pandemic, the pace of translation projects has accelerated, partly due to new technology. Now, there are only 1,300 languages remaining to translate. It's still a lot, of course, but it's a tenfold increase in the pace of new projects starting. Isn't that amazing?

Today, we can praise God that his word is so widely available to us and around the world. We can read it by ourselves, with our friends, or in churches and gatherings. We can listen to audio Bibles. We can find podcasts and sermons on every book of the Bible. We can read commentaries extensively or google answers to our difficult questions. We can watch the Bible Project explain the history, context and authorship of each section. We can study theology in depth at Bible colleges in every state and country of the world. But most of all, we can sit quietly with the words of the Bible and let God speak to us personally, convicting, comforting and encouraging us through his word and his Spirit. What a wonderful time to be alive.

5
'I knew it to be true'

There's another profound aspect to many people's faith stories that I noticed in various forms as I listened. Alongside the unravelling, the personal need, the questions, the friendly contacts, the invitations to churches, the reading of the Bible and the grappling with God's truth and Lordship over many years, there was often an unexplainable moment that occurred in the middle of it all.

The person said to me, 'I suddenly knew in my heart that it was true.'

They couldn't necessarily tell me why or how, or even exactly when it happened. They had no rational explanation. They couldn't even say how it felt, using any further verbs or adjectives. They merely described a moment of knowing, deeply and without a doubt, that it was true. Scott said it happened in a split second. Both Edgar and Karen said that it was like a light switching on. Bec and Memo likened it to scales falling from their eyes. They knew God was real. They knew God loved them. They knew God sent his Son, the Lord Jesus, to die for them. They knew they were forgiven. And they responded.

In every case, it was more than reading about truth in the Bible. It was more than hearing a cleverly exposed sermon or absorbing the words in a well-crafted Christian book or podcast and agreeing intellectually. It was more than the powerful prayer of a friend or relative. It was more than the deep love of a church or the persuasion of a respected pastor.

It was the Holy Spirit at work in their own hearts in a way that they couldn't explain. They said that in that moment, they suddenly knew it to be true. Jesus was real, and they responded.

This is actually my favourite part of every interview and story. Whenever I hear it, I pause, smile and thank God profoundly for the amazing way he moves the human soul. It feels like a sacred moment to me – the fact that God's Spirit chooses to work in us and reveal himself so beautifully, unmistakably and irrevocably. It's exactly as we read in Jesus' words in John 6:44: 'No one can come to me unless the Father who sent me draws them ...'

Of course, not everybody described to me one single moment in time. For some people, there were many moments of assurance over many years. I wonder ... if we were to stop right now and ask ourselves the questions, 'Do I believe in God? Is he real? Has Jesus paid my debts? Am I sure?' we would probably answer, 'Yes!'

But how do we know *for sure*? Is it more than biblical exposition, the historicity of Jesus and the persuasion of sermons and gifted preachers? Did we know *for sure* yesterday and last year? Will we know *for sure* next week and next year, even within our doubts? How will we know *for sure*, deep in our hearts?

Let me introduce **Alan**, who is the father of one of our good friends. Alan knew, for sure, suddenly, that Jesus was real when he was aged 52. Alan's daughter regularly tells me that after that moment, Alan's life absolutely changed.

> 'My father was killed in a quarry accident when I was 14. He was leaning over the mudguard, attending to the engine of his five-tonne tip truck when another vehicle, carelessly driven,

crushed his body, spine and ribs. He suffered for four hours and then he died. I only saw him briefly in the hospital. I remember my mother sobbing. Whilst I knew my dad loved me, he never displayed affection. There was no touching. And I'd had a row with him the previous night. I felt guilty for a long time.

I was the eldest of five children, and the youngest was only 13 months old, so I left school and got an apprenticeship. I had a couple of breakdowns. As an adult, I started drinking heavily to escape the pain. Alcoholics can be private people. I didn't want anyone to know about the drinking, so I would sneak alcohol into the house and hide it in the garage. But I think my daughter knew. She could hear it or smell it.

Along the way, I probably heard about Jesus, but I didn't pay any attention. My wife was a Christian, and we went to church, but nothing stuck for me. I felt like I was hiding not just the alcohol but the fact that I wasn't a Christian.

Then, when I was 52, a pastor came to our house and he tried to do Christianity Explained with me. I still didn't pay attention. I had my mind elsewhere. But the following week, the assistant pastor came to our house and he prayed with me a few times. While he was praying, something happened. The penny suddenly dropped. I felt Christ's presence. I knew it was true! I felt Jesus smiling at me. I knew that he was a real person and that he died for my sins. I'd been fighting it the whole time, but it was true. Everything fell into place. I can't explain it to you except that the Lord did something in me.

> Giving up drinking and smoking is never easy. For me, though, it was a complete change, virtually overnight. It was like I'd walked through the wardrobe into Narnia. I gave up drinking straight away. I knew that I was forgiven. Jesus gave his life for me. I'd been forgiven by him, so I could forgive my father, and I could even forgive myself. It was instant relief. I suddenly realised that Jesus suffered far more than I did. It says in 1 Peter 3:18, "For Christ also suffered once for sins, the righteous for the unrighteous, to bring you to God." It meant that, for me, I didn't have to carry the weight of sadness and guilt anymore. Jesus had taken it for me.
>
> Straight away, I started going to Bible study. And I talked about my faith with everyone I met. I didn't hide it! I still talk to everyone I meet, even now, and I tell them what Jesus has done for me, even if I meet them in a lift or at the podiatrist!'

As humans, we carry guilt and pain, sometimes for decades or even a lifetime. It can feel like our cells absorb it, and there is no escape. Sometimes, we are drawn to any kind of deadening or numbing process, which then becomes a new, hidden burden. But, wonderfully, in Alan's case, after years of attending church and not understanding any of it, his assistant pastor visited, prayed for him and suddenly the penny dropped. Alan knew, for sure, that Jesus died for him and was with him. He just knew! He can't describe how he knew in that moment, but he knows that he did.

I love the fact that the truth of the gospel brought about such immediate change in Alan's heart, not just in his outer life and habits but in his thinking regarding forgiveness. He knew he was forgiven by God, and because of that great mercy, he could forgive himself. He became a person who now shares his faith with everyone he meets. Having spent time with Alan, I can vouch for this! He's a delight, often talking persuasively to everyone he meets about his new faith.

Of course, coming to faith in Jesus doesn't always magically change our habits or addictions overnight, as it did in Alan's case. It can be a long, slow process of trusting Jesus with our pain and continuing to get help in various forms. But our faith gives us new hope, and that new hope slowly begins to change our neural pathways. We can rest in the knowledge that we have been utterly loved, forgiven and shown grace. Christ suffered for us to bring us to God. We can forgive ourselves, forgive each other and overflow with the goodness of God and what Christ has done for us. May that be the case in our lives today.

§

I mentioned before that there is power in songs and worship music. Like prayer, God often uses the gift of songs and lyrics to speak to our hearts. An example is **Lily**. She said she had a single moment when the Holy Spirit worked in her heart. In that moment, she knew for sure that God loved her. But in her case, the moment was connected to an old, almost-forgotten line in a hymn.

> 'I was raised by a single parent – my mum. She did her best, but my childhood was unstable and, at times, unsafe. We moved around a lot. I think my impression, as a kid, was that the whole world seemed unstable.
>
> At five years old, I remember I went to a Scripture class at school. I was sitting on the floor, looking up at my teacher,

whose name was Mrs Bubble. She said that God was real and in control of everything. The world was controlled by God! I'd never heard about God before, except as a swear word, so I thought it was super cool. Then she said that if anyone wanted to learn more about God, the place to go was church.

That afternoon, my grandmother picked me up from school and I told her there was a God who loved me, and that I wanted to go to church. From then on, Grandma and I started going to a little church at the end of her street, every Sunday. It was stable and consistent, in my unstable world, which was what I craved.

But in my teens, life became even more complex and difficult. My mum had three more kids, and I assisted with them. I began to attribute all of the bad things in my life to God. If he was in charge, then everything was clearly all his fault. My behaviour and mental health spiralled. I had frequent angry outbursts, and I was aggressive and unkind … an awful person to be around! I would still tell people I was a Christian, but my behaviour was the opposite of the fruits of the Spirit.

Then, when I was 15, my mum had a severe stroke in front of me. I called the ambulance. It impacted her mobility and memory, so afterwards we were put in the care of Grandma, who was in her early 70s by then. It turned the dial up to 100. I became even more unstable, and I vented my anger on everyone.

But I still had one close friend who was a Christian. One day, we were hanging out in a public space, and I was describing my drinking and promiscuity. She said, "Maybe you shouldn't call yourself a Christian if you're behaving like that?"

I lost it. I got really angry with her, and I cut off all ties. At the same time, I was given a diagnosis of complex post-traumatic stress disorder as a result of my childhood. I remember going home, sitting on the floor of my shower and crying. I'd never gone to God with my distress before, but that day I did.

After the shower, I started singing "Rock of Ages" absentmindedly. It was an old song I knew from going to church as a child. Then something happened. My brain turned on. What are you singing, and why? Do you know what a "cleft" is?

For me, it happened in an instant. I went from saying that everything was God's fault to knowing for sure that God was my refuge. He was trustworthy and safe. I could go to him in my pain. He loved me! Jesus had given up his life for me! It was all that mattered. So, I said to God, "I'm sorry. I didn't know who you were, or what you had done for me."

My life slowly changed. I apologised to my friend, and I started listening at church. I read Titus 2:14 and thought about what it means to be "eager" to do what God wants – to find great joy in it. That really changed my mindset over time. Then after school, I did Year 13 with Youthworks, which was great. Today, God continues to shape me into Christlikeness, and he also helps me navigate my mental health challenges. I'm married to the kindest man in the world. But more than that, it's the Holy Spirit who is at work in my life, shaping me, even within my ongoing brokenness. It's incredible!'

I love that Lily said she came to God in her brokenness and found her safe place in him, her cleft in the rock. I also love that she described that single moment when she was at her worst. She was crying in the shower and then suddenly began singing, absentmindedly. As she sang, the Holy Spirit worked in her heart, and she profoundly realised that God loved her. In that moment, she put her trust in Jesus as her only refuge and safe place. Over time, God changed her. Her story makes me thankful for Scripture teachers like Mrs Bubble and grandmothers who take their grandchildren to church, even when they're probably exhausted or would prefer to be doing something else.

Lily's story also highlights the issues of safety and security. As humans, we tend to do whatever we can to make our lives safe, secure and stable. For Lily, that longed-for security was at its most basic level – food, a place to stay and the absence of harm. Her story hints at the truth that even the most basic provisions were not always available to her, which is a terrible, unimaginable burden to carry.

For many of us, our search for security has more complex layers, such as accumulating skills, undergoing medical check-ups, making contingency plans, securing ample superannuation or managing relational expectations. We pursue security, but every day we realise that our bodies and family lives are fragile. We are not immune to a shaky world, a changing environment, systems of injustice and the upheaval of our own hearts. We too can come to God in our worst moments and find our deepest sense of refuge and safety in our relationship with him. He is with us. He is our cleft in the rock. *Lord, we thank you for who you are. Help us to rest in you rather than in all the easier answers that lie nearby.*

§

For Lily, she cried out to God in song in her worst moment and had an immediate assurance of his presence, which was wonderful. He was her refuge! The Holy Spirit worked in her heart. However, prior to that, Lily had already heard about God. She had been to church with her grandma and acknowledged that God probably existed. But for some of us, like our friend **Geoff**, the situation was different. Geoff was adamant that God *didn't* exist! Yet, he cried out anyway and was very surprised ...

> 'At 21, I went overseas with the wrong crowd. We were in Europe in winter, using drugs and chasing women. Then we came home via Afghanistan, also doing the same thing. I lost all meaning ... and it continued when I got back to Australia.
>
> Eventually, I ended up in a psychiatric hospital at age 24. But even after that, I didn't always take my medication. I was in and out of hospital until I was at death's door at age 32. I'd lost all hope. I'd tried everything except the right way.
>
> And that's when I cried out to God at 2 am.
>
> I just said, "God, help me!"
>
> And I suddenly felt his presence. I wasn't even expecting it. I just cried out to him because I couldn't think of anything else to do. God was real. It was such a surprise!
>
> But in that moment, I felt there was hope. My aunt was a Catholic nun, and she invited me to the convent the next week. I prayed there. After that, I went to a local church and I heard people praying. I thought they were crazy, but I went back the next week and I responded to an altar call. I gave my life to Jesus.

> Since then, it hasn't always been easy. But I like Romans 10:13, which says, "Everyone who calls on the name of the Lord will be saved." It's really true! We can call out to God and he hears us, even when we least expect him to! And I know that God knows ... everything.'

Isn't that lovely? There was Geoff, in the hospital, at death's door, with no hope and no more options. He cried out to God, almost offhandedly, because he couldn't think of anything else to say or do. And God answered him! It was the last thing Geoff expected.

It's wonderful because it's so unexpected. It reminds me a bit of Bec and Memo's story back in chapter 2. They, too, were suddenly and unexpectedly convicted of the reality of God, which was the last thing they expected at the marriage weekend. I find it challenging, perhaps because sometimes I'm tempted to think that God's response to my requests or cries depends on how fervent or faith-filled my cry is. But Geoff cried out to God, not even believing that God existed ... and God answered him. God's replies are not contingent on our faith or fervency (although there's nothing wrong with fervency). God will answer in his ways, in his timing, for his purposes. His ways are not our ways, and neither are his thoughts our thoughts, as it says so beautifully in Isaiah 55:8. I often need to re-read that truth! *Lord, we thank you today that your thoughts are not our thoughts, and your ways are not our ways. Please help us to call out to you again, in any way we can.*

§

Let's have one more example of a sudden, momentary awareness that Jesus is absolutely present and Lord of our lives. I first met **Roseamanda** through a mutual friend living in Alice Springs. I

5. 'I knew it to be true'

immediately loved her passion and her honesty. She is someone who now bubbles over with her love of Jesus and the way he has changed her life. Roseamanda told me about a single moment in time at a church in Alice Springs in 2021.

> 'I was a really heavy drinker and smoker. I was gambling at the casino and at the pubs, like that – drinking so much. I used to sleep on the hospital lawn sometimes – yeah, I was homeless. I have two daughters and one son. My other son passed away. It was really not good – that life, all the things I was doing. I wasn't feeling good. I had a caseworker.
>
> She said to me, "Where are you staying?"
>
> I said, "I'm sleeping on the hospital lawn."
>
> Then she said, "You can't do that. I'm going to move you into a hostel."
>
> When I moved there to the hostel, I was still drinking and going to parties, living for myself, going back drunk to the hostel and doing rubbish things. One day, I sat down. I had a hangover. Everything I did – sleeping, walking – felt really heavy in my head. That's when I noticed my Auntie Rosie walking past. It was a Sunday, in the middle of March last year, 2021.
>
> I said, "Auntie, where are you going?"
>
> She said, "I'm going to church."
>
> I said, "I'm coming with you!"
>
> From then on, round about the 21st March last year, I went to that church. One day, the Holy Spirit changed me. I felt that

God was there. I got down on my knees and gave my life to Jesus. I received healing. Praise God!

About a month later, though, I was still smoking. My cousin saw it and he said, "I thought you were going to the church?"

I began to think in my mind. I thought my smoking was blocking the way for the Holy Spirit. I wanted Jesus to touch my cousin. So I went to my room and I picked up all the smokes and I threw them in the rubbish bin. Jesus helped me, praise the Lord!

That was in April last year. Twelve months later, I haven't stopped praising God. I haven't touched the smokes or the drink. During the week, I go to church. I also do outreach at the hospital. I weep and cry for my people – for God to bring them from darkness to light. I tell them, "God loves you." Jesus loves you. He died on the cross for you. He shed his blood for you, for all of us.

I've been in hospital myself, and also my daughter was in the hospital. She gave birth to a small premmie baby. I stayed in the hospital with her too. While I was there, I told the nurses about Jesus. I prayed for them. And I prayed for the baby. The baby got better really quickly! He went from the humidicrib to the cot, and then into his mother's arms. It was quicker than they thought.

They said, "This baby should have been here for months! How come it's so quick?"

I said, "I been praying!" Praise the Lord.

5. 'I knew it to be true'

> My favourite verse is Romans 6:23. "For the wages of sin is death, but the gift of God is eternal life in Christ Jesus our Lord." I read it in English and Walpiri and Pitjantjatjara. I also sing a song, "I Have Decided To Follow Jesus." I want to tell all the people, God loves you. God created you in his own image. God is so amazing!'

Roseamanda is brimming over with her love for Jesus! That single moment in church changed her life. I especially appreciated her description of it. It wasn't long or theological. She merely said that she felt God was there, got down on her knees and gave her life to Jesus. The Holy Spirit changed her! I also love the way she speaks now, often holding her brown leather Bible close to her chest, rejoicing in the truths she has found in it and wanting to share them with everyone.

Hearing Roseamanda's story also makes me feel challenged and humbled in my own journey. What would it mean for me to submit to God within all the things that still distract and consume me? What would it mean for me to bubble over with the outrageous love of God? What would it mean for me to weep and cry for my friends and neighbours, including those at the hospital? What would it mean for me to pray earnestly and expectantly for those in need, like Roseamanda does?

Mostly, hearing stories like Roseamanda's and all the others like hers have made me deeply thankful for the wonderful, transformative work of the Holy Spirit in each of our lives, in single moments and over decades. It makes me plead with the Holy Spirit to stir our hearts, right now, in surprising ways, and to help us deepen our trust in Jesus. May we each be people who follow Jesus whole-heartedly, without turning back or hedging our bets, or all the other things we do regularly. May we each be people who love to point to Jesus, in our ordinary lives, and expect him to answer!

6
Beautiful exceptions

In the previous chapters, I have focused on the patterns I have seen in 300 faith stories. These patterns are important and valuable because they teach us much and encourage us to continue praying for God's work in the hearts of our friends and relatives. Observing these patterns makes us more expectant, helping us to notice both the unravelling and the way God provides through trusted friends, his Word and his Spirit. However, I also began this book by noting the most wonderful aspect of gathering so many faith stories: the great *variety* amidst surprising patterns. Every story I heard was different and unique!

In this chapter, I want to share some beautiful exceptions to these patterns, just in case you're beginning to think that God always follows a recipe. Nothing could be further from the truth!

Our Western, scientific mindset often inclines us to believe that God only works in ways that seem rational or understandable to us. We know that God speaks through his Word, his Spirit and through trusted, faithful friends, etc. Yet, we must be careful not to limit God or his revelation to us through miracles and unexplainable phenomena. Even in Australia, God speaks to us through dreams, visions and other utterly surprising events and circumstances.

Perhaps like me, you've heard stories of these kinds of events happening regularly in Asia, the Middle East and Africa. That's true too. During our years living in Nepal, Darren and I frequently heard accounts from our Nepali friends about how they came to faith in Jesus through miracles or visions. For example, our friend Pratima grew up in an isolated Hindu village in western Nepal. One day, her mother had a vision of Jesus, dressed in white with his arms outstretched. The whole family came to faith in Christ and began attending the local Christian church in their village. Another friend, Bishnu Maya, was very unwell with typhoid in her late teens, in a Hindu village without a doctor. Alone and desperate, she prayed to Jesus and was miraculously healed. From that day on, she trusted in Jesus, and her faith spread to the rest of her family.

I could tell you many similar stories. When Darren and I travelled through Iraq, China, Tibet, Kyrgyzstan and India, collecting stories for *The Plum Tree in the Desert* and *Finding Faith*, we heard many testimonies of God revealing himself through dreams and visions.

There's a tendency amongst Western, conservative Christians to think that such phenomena are confined to places like Nepal, where access to the Bible is limited or cultural norms differ significantly. While this may be true to some extent, after interviewing hundreds of people in Australia, I have realised that God also uses dreams, visions, audible voices and other surprising phenomena here to direct people's attention to himself.

Here is **Chris**'s story.

> 'I grew up in Launceston. When I was 17, I joined the Tasmanian police force, and after training, they gave me a gun and a badge and said, 'Go and do it.' I really loved my job,

and I did every aspect of policing over the next 20 years. I also met a lovely lady, Debbie, and we got married and had our first child. Life was good.

But back in the day, in the 80s, when serious incidents happened, there was no counselling or debriefing. The boss would just say, "Go home and have a stubbie – you'll be right."

An incident happened in 1992 that really tipped me over the edge. I arrested and charged a man for three offences in one night. A few days later, the man rang the station, and the call went through to my home. My wife answered it, and the man said he was coming around to shoot me.

I became very stressed. I slept with my gun under my pillow. My job was on my mind 24/7, and eventually I had a breakdown. I lost all my confidence.

Afterwards, I was on sick leave for two years. I had a good Christian doctor, though, who was very supportive of me. During that time, I built a house on our farm … and as the house grew, my confidence started to grow.

But after two years, I still wasn't able to work as a police officer. They gave me a plaque and said thanks for coming. I became very depressed and angry. My wife put up with a lot, but she was wonderfully supportive. She was a Christian and she was praying for me.

On the 1st of April 1994, I went out the back door, into the paddock, and I just yelled at God. I said, "God, are you real? I'm a cop and I need evidence! So, give me proof! Prove to me the Bible is real! Also, people say that I need a relationship with Jesus. Well, give me that as well!"

I went back inside. Sixteen days later, on a Saturday night, I was thinking, "Well, where are you, God? You haven't fronted up."

Just then, I heard an audible voice behind me saying, "John."

My head nearly snapped off my shoulders. There was no one else there. I said, "Is that you, God?"

I remembered that "John" was a book in the New Testament, so I said to God, "Do you want me to read it? Whereabouts do you want me to read?"

You won't believe this, but on the wall above me, appeared three numbers: 211. I was excited. I said to God, "Is that chapter 2, verse 11?" As I said it, the numbers disappeared from the wall.

The week before that, my wife had actually bought me a Bible. She said, "This is for you. If you ever want to read it, it's sitting over here on the table."

Back then, I said, "No way!" But something happened inside me on that Saturday night, and I knew I wanted to read John 2:11, so I found the Bible.

The verse said, "Jesus performed this first miracle in Cana in Galilee; there he revealed his glory, and his disciples believed in him" [GNT].

It hit me. It was a miracle. I believed in Jesus, in that moment! I felt the weight come off my shoulders, and I felt full of joy. I hadn't felt joy for years.

> I went to my wife and told her. I was jumping around, full of joy. She was calm. She said that years earlier, she'd had a similar experience of God speaking to her.
>
> I said, "Why didn't you tell me?"
>
> She said, "You weren't ready."
>
> And she was right. She was always right. That was the beginning of my 29-year journey with Jesus. I had a Good News Bible and I consumed it all. It was wonderful. It was a tremendous time of growth. I'd been transformed and I was a new creation. The weight of depression, anger and alcoholism fell from my shoulders. We ended up having eight children, four of our own and four adopted children from Ethiopia. Of course, there have been ups and downs in the last 29 years, but overall, it's been fabulous.'

Isn't that amazing? Chris, being a cop, wanted hard evidence and asked God for proof. He demanded to be shown something, and God showed him something! As Chris described it to me, 29 years after the actual event, I could still hear the shock in his voice. He asked for proof and was gobsmacked when he actually heard God speak in an audible voice and saw writing on the wall.

But alongside the strange and unexplainable events in this story, God also worked through more 'normal' ways – through his word in the Bible, specifically John 2:10; through Chris' faithful, praying wife, and through Chris' Christian doctor. The whole story is beautiful. More than anything, it reminds me that God can and does speak in whichever way he chooses, in his timing, to turn our hearts to himself.

Of course, God doesn't always provide clear, visible answers when we demand them of him. He is God, after all, and can choose to reveal himself in his own ways and timing. If he doesn't do it in the way we want, it doesn't mean he isn't listening or present. But we are allowed (and even invited) to be honest with him, which is another encouragement we glean from Chris' story. It's okay to be honest with God and to tell him exactly what we're thinking at every stage of life. Being God, of course, he already knows. He invites us to come to him with all our groanings, laments, angry questions and heartache, as well as our delight, thanksgiving and joy.

It's also wonderful that God directed Chris immediately back to his word in the Bible. *Lord, help us also to be people who look to you, without limitation, and who respond honestly to your gracious invitation, today.*

§

In Chris's case, he asked God for proof and received it unexpectedly. In many cases, though, people are continuing along with their lives, not actually asking God for anything or even acknowledging him at all, and then suddenly, God appears. That was the case for our friend **Jeremy**.

> 'In 2014, I had a Damascus Road experience ... well, a Mosman Road experience. At the time, I had long stopped caring about the God of my childhood. Instead, I was in a long-term battle with addiction and depression. No matter how long I stayed clean or sober, I inevitably fell back into old habits. I couldn't stop, and I felt like I had tried everything. I was pretty sure that eventually my wife would leave me. I'd most likely give in to getting wasted all the time, and then

probably die young and alone. That was about the extent of my plans ... until the Lord intervened.

It was very early on a Sunday morning, probably about 2 am. I was walking home after post-work festivities at a mate's house. I hadn't got far when a voice called my name, saying, "Jeremy, stop." I looked around and there was no one, so I kept walking, and the voice said it again. It seemed to speak to my very core. So, I listened; I stopped. Then my legs went weak, and with tears streaming down my face, I had to sit down. I didn't know what was going on, but at the same time, I knew my Father's voice. The last 10 years flashed before my eyes, all the terrible things I'd done ... I wept bitterly.

"It's okay," he reassured me. My tears slowed, and I felt something I hadn't felt for a long time ... peace. It was as if I was basking in the presence of God! I eventually reached our apartment, and as I walked in the door, my wife called out, "Are you okay?" "I think I saw God," was all I could say, before I started bawling like a baby. As she prayed for me, I realised ... God wouldn't let me go. So, I handed myself over. "I'm all yours," I said, "do with me what you will."

It'd be nice to say that from that moment on everything was totally different, but this is not a fairytale – it's the story of a broken man. Over the next six months my life felt like a contradiction. On one hand I now went to church because I wanted to, and I joined a Bible study, but at the same time, I continued to fall into my old habits, behaving at times like nothing had ever happened. One night after work again, I cried out to the Lord and he said, "Go read your Bible." I had no idea where to start, but 'Romans' popped into my head ... so I began to read, and it was like I could finally see. I read chapters 1–3 slowly, at times unable to drink in all that it offered. It brought forth floods of tears as well as exclamations of joy. In that moment, it gave me the answers to every question I was asking and showed me why I am the way I am, why the world is as it is, but most importantly, that God in his mercy had solved these problems through his son Jesus Christ!

Since then, there have been times when it felt like overnight, I became a totally different person, a new creation, full of the Holy Spirit. But at other times it feels like nothing has changed, and that I'm destined to struggle and fail for the rest of my days. Even so, I must remember that the Lord is faithful and will never let me go, and he is working in all the messiness of life ... somehow, for the good of those who love him, including me.'

I love Jeremy's honesty. We need to hear that. He says the Lord worked powerfully in his life on that early Sunday morning while he was walking home from work – telling him to stop and then providing deep comfort and reassurance. It's an amazing story. The way God stopped Jeremy in his tracks, so much so that he had to sit down, is remarkable. Additionally, God worked through Jeremy's prayerful, patient wife, and he continues to work in Jeremy's life in an ongoing way.

But it's also refreshing for us to hear Jeremy's honesty. He admits that since that night in Mosman, his ongoing journey hasn't been a fairytale. It's been slow and hard, as it has been for many of us. Jeremy admits brokenness, confusion and the habits of the human soul. And we are all like Jeremy. We would rather it was quicker and smoother.

We would rather have a fairytale! But instead, we come to God in our honesty, confusion and brokenness. We too have faced the reality of our frail condition, and we come, often, in weakness and repentance. In return, we are offered sweet, undeserved grace.

It's so much better than a fairytale. Jesus took on the curse of sin himself. And while the process of becoming more and more Christlike can seem long and arduous, or as if we're moving backwards or limping along, falling into the same unhelpful patterns, we are not discouraged. We cling on. The Spirit's work is gentle as well as astute. God is faithful. He knows what we need, and he uses his word to speak into our souls in all the ways he knows we need today, as we come to him. We continue to receive grace freely. *Lord, we thank you that we can come to you again today, honestly, stumbling, but overwhelmingly grateful for your sweet, undeserved grace.*

§

Something that keeps featuring in these stories is the recognisability of Jesus' voice. Jeremy heard God's voice in Mosman and immediately knew it was the Lord, even though he wasn't expecting him to speak. Chris heard God's voice in his home and immediately knew it was him. The story that follows is from our friend **Norm**, who lives in Adelaide. Norm also heard a voice and knew straight away that it was Jesus. Not only that, but God performed a miracle in Norm's heart overnight.

> 'In 1988, I'd gone through some years of having a real issue with anger. Any small thing could set me off. I was that touchy. It culminated in 1988, when I was 39. A lot of negative things happened and put a strain on our marriage. My grandmother

died and my father died. Both our dogs died. We had to sell our house in Adelaide, and we were housesitting. It all intensified my anger. One night I was so angry I couldn't sleep. Someone had said something to me the day before. I can't remember what it was now, but it set me off. I was lying in bed, and I was so angry that I was shaking.

Then suddenly, out of the blue, Jesus spoke to me. He said, "If you turn to me, everything will be different."

At first, I argued with him. I didn't agree. But then, I said, "Okay, I believe in you, Jesus."

I went to sleep and when I woke up, everything was completely different. I knew I was different. The kind of black anger that I'd been feeling for all those years just went away and it never returned. I've never experienced it again.

Before that point, I'd had very little Christian influence. My parents sent me to Sunday school and church when I was younger, but I stopped going when I was 13. My wife had a similar background. But I knew the voice was Jesus. I was so sure of it. At the same time as the voice, there was an amazing light in the centre of my mind. It was visibly there when the voice spoke and not there before or afterwards.

It took my wife six months before she agreed the anger had really gone. At first, she thought I could be faking it. But after six months, she realised it was for real. I was different.

We started going to church together. It was a life-changing time. My faith in Jesus was such a precious gift. It was a living relationship! We talked with the minister, and we saw a lot of answered prayer during those early years. Sometimes it was as simple as a hymn in my head that encouraged me or praying for my wife at work at the exact time she needed it.

After a few years, people started asking us whether we were interested in overseas mission. I was struck by the truth found in John 3:16. God loved the whole world (with all its sin and muck), so he gave his one and only Son, for all the people, not just for those nearby. One day I was sitting at work, and I got a clear indication from God that it was time to start preparing for overseas mission. I signed up for Bible college, and then we left for the Middle East. We spent five years there, involved in a whole range of ministries.

I've always really liked Ephesians 2:8–10. "For it is by grace you have been saved, through faith – and this is not from yourselves, it is the gift of God – not by works, so that no one can boast. For we are God's handiwork, created in Christ Jesus to do good works, which God prepared in advance for us to do."

When Jesus came into my life, it was such a precious gift. It was life-changing, in a wonderful way, and it made me want to serve. Even now, I've just come out of hospital, and I can't do what I used to do, but I know Jesus always has a role for us to play. We'll always be doing something that God has prepared for us to do!'

Like Jeremy and Chris, Norm knew without a doubt that the voice he was hearing was Jesus. At 39, he hadn't had any Christian influence since he was 13, but as soon as God spoke to him that night, Norm recognised God's voice and responded. I find this tremendously encouraging. We have all been made in the image of God, by God, for God. We are his creation and his delight. We are like his clay pots, formed in his own hand, wonderfully and fearfully, albeit cracked. So, of course, when God speaks to us, we will stop in our tracks and respond to him, unequivocally – even when we're not expecting him, even when we're distracted, even when we're mired in our own anger and even if we've never heard the name of Jesus before. We are created to know his voice!

In Norm's case, it's also interesting that when he heard God's voice, it was accompanied by a shining light in the centre of his mind. Norm must have been overwhelmed by that light in contrast to his own black anger. It's a helpful reminder that God's voice (through his word and in every other way) will always be ultimately hopeful. It will always bring light and healing to our souls. It will never bring further despair or darkness. How could it?

Even more amazingly, in Norm's case, God worked in his heart overnight as he slept, such that when he woke up, his intense anger had gone, never to return. It's such a wonderful, transformative testimony to the power of God, even as we sleep. I also love the side note that it took Norm's wife, Maggie, six months to believe that he wasn't faking it. But then she did believe him, and they've been serving Jesus together wholeheartedly for 33 years, in all the ways that God prepared for them.

Lastly, I love Norm's favourite verse from Ephesians 2. In all the 300 interviews I did, I always asked the person for a favourite Bible verse. Interestingly, there was such a range of beautiful responses, which thrilled my heart. Hardly any two verses were the same. Everybody also explained to me the way God had used those living words in

6. Beautiful exceptions

their hearts and lives over time. To me, it seems absolutely fitting that Norm's favourite verse is Ephesians 2:8-10. He was saved by grace, not by works. He was saved by God's merciful work in his life, rather than anything he did. He didn't do anything! He simply acknowledged Jesus as Lord, and then went to sleep. No wonder Norm has spent 33 years since then talking about the precious gift of God in his life. May we also be people who are overwhelmed again by the grace of God at work in our lives and in the world that he so deeply loves. May we remember daily that we are God's handiwork, created in Christ Jesus to do the works he has already prepared for us to do.

§

While we're thinking about the shining light of God's truth and presence, I'd like you to meet our friend **Michael**. Michael came to faith in Jesus as a young person, but then 50 years later, he had an experience of God's truth and light that shaped him in new and deeper ways.

> 'My father did a lot of travelling for work. We didn't see him much. And then one day, he just didn't come home. He left for good. I left school and I got work in the timber yard, so I could pay off the mortgage on the family home. Dad had gone and if I didn't do it, we'd have no roof over our heads.
>
> Then one day, a cousin of a schoolmate knocked on my door, and he said, "Would you like to go to Bible study?"
>
> I said, "All right, I'll give it a go."
>
> Then later, he said, "Would you like to go to church?"
>
> I said the same thing, "All right, I'll give it a go."

From the beginning, it just felt right. It was true. Jesus died for us.

In Bible study one day, we read in 1 John 1:5 about Jesus being the light. Then we were asked whether we'd rather walk in the light (following Jesus) or in the darkness. Well, the light, of course! I've been growing in my faith since then, little bit by little bit.

But, in 2016, when I was in my 70s, I wasn't feeling well. I had chest pains, and my wife called an ambulance. Half an hour later, I had a cardiac arrest in the emergency department of the hospital. I was lying on the hospital bed in a brightly lit room, and all of a sudden everything went dark.

But in the darkness, there was one bright light shining, high above me.

My first thought was, "They haven't paid the electricity bill."

But then, at the same time, I felt a peace all through me – every part of me. It was fantastic! I didn't want it to stop. I wanted to stay like that. But then the darkness slowly left, and the lights came back on, and a nurse woke me up. I didn't want her to! I wanted to stay there, with that one bright light and the peace!

Since then, I've been different. I needed heart surgery (five bypasses) that year, but it didn't rattle me. I knew the peace of God, and I knew that whether I came out of the operations or if I didn't, everything would be fine. Death is not the problem. I know that I'll be with God (because of Jesus) and it will be good. I will have that peace!'

6. Beautiful exceptions

Isn't that lovely? God is able to surprise us with his presence, comfort and truth throughout our lives, sometimes miraculously, and even when we're close to death. Perhaps God reveals himself to us even more at the end? I've certainly heard quite a few accounts similar to Michael's, where people have seen shining lights and experienced bright hope in near-death encounters, knowing for sure that God is real and present. The beautiful outcome is that, afterwards, when the person recovers, they usually describe a closer walk with Jesus and a deeper trust that everything is ultimately okay. God is in control. For Michael, the experience meant he had a new peace and perspective as he faced multiple serious heart operations. He knew that no matter what happened, whether he lived or died, he would be with God. *Lord, we ask today that we too would have that same assurance and perspective, no matter how close we are to the end of our days here on earth. Please remind us that eternity awaits!*

§

So far, the beautiful exceptions in this chapter have mostly included stories of God speaking in miraculous and unexpected ways, which is wonderful. **Russ**'s story is quite different. I'd love you to read it because his response to a time of unravelling was unexpected, even to him. He didn't become angry, questioning or desperate. Instead, he wanted someone to thank. Coming from an atheist background, he had no one.

> 'In my 30s, I had a plan for my life. There was no way God figured in it. I was reading a fair bit of personal development literature out of the United States – for example, *The Power of Positive Thinking*. I liked the book, but as soon as the author

mentioned God, I put it down. That's it. The author is not valid. He's off with the pixies.

My dad was an atheist and a member of the Communist Party of Australia. We grew up with that background. I also went to a fairly academic high school that encouraged us to think logically and scientifically.

But right through my teens, I had this fascination with the person of Jesus. I couldn't refute that he was a historical figure. I used to listen to the musical *Jesus Christ, Superstar* and sing along with the lyrics. But my logical brain wouldn't accept the divinity thing. I didn't believe in God!

From 20 to 40, I didn't give Christ another hearing. I did, however, notice a lot of hypocrites in the church. They put me off. I also saw the different denominations throwing rocks at each other, which also put me off. Christianity must be a lot of rot if the denominations are behaving like that.

Then a whole bunch of things happened in 1993. A lady came into my office asking questions about my work. As she left, she said, "The hand of God must be on you." I didn't know how to react. She encouraged me to go to church. I didn't. But I've never forgotten what she said.

Then, later that year, I was diagnosed with bowel cancer, out of the blue. I was 40 years old, and we had three young kids and a business. I burst into tears. I'd never been confronted with my mortality before. It was a sudden, random detection. I had no outward signs, but it was 10 days from being diagnosed to going under the knife.

6. Beautiful exceptions

After I got out of hospital, I was sitting on a bench on the main street of Springwood, in the Blue Mountains, west of Sydney. I was feeling thankful to be alive ... As I was sitting there, a work colleague walked past. He stopped and we talked. He was really concerned for me.

I told him that I felt like saying thank you to God ... whom I didn't know ... and I had no idea how to say thank you to God.

He said, "I'll pick you up on Sunday."

That Sunday we trotted off to church together. Afterwards, he took me under his wing and started to answer my questions. He was amazingly helpful. He said that Christianity is about following Christ, it's not about following other Christians. He also said I needed to work out whether Jesus is who he said he is.

I started reading the New Testament – the Gospels and Acts – as well as books by Josh McDowell. I devoured all of it. It was fascinating – all these lives were absolutely transformed by Jesus: the disciples, Stephen and Paul. Something really big must have happened.

I understood it historically, but I kept having arguments with God, especially about accepting him as my boss. If I submitted it to him, I might have to do as he said. I also didn't understand why Jesus had to die. I didn't see myself as a sinful man, back then. I thought humanity was essentially good.

But then I read Romans 3. Actually, no one is good enough: "... for all have sinned and fall short of the glory of God" (v. 23).

In the months after that, when I looked back at history, including communism and socialism, it made more sense! We aren't

> good, any of us, and we need the grace of God. In October 1994, I submitted to Jesus. I prayed, "Jesus, you're the Lord. Please take over my life."
>
> In the next few years, all our three kids started coming to church with me, and then my wife. It was a slow process of change in all of us.
>
> Now, I want to say to people, "Don't leave it too late. Don't be regretful. We don't know how long we have. Don't waste the years of your youth!" I want to encourage people to have the tough arguments with God early on, while they can. And I praise God for the tough stuff in my life. In my case, my cancer drew me to God.'

Russ wonderfully describes so many of the elements of God at work in our lives that we've seen in previous chapters – his contact at work, the friend who took him to church, the power of God's word, the questions, the moment when it all made sense and the ripple effect in his family. However, I wanted to include Russ's story in this chapter because of the unique aspect of thanksgiving. As humans, we are wired to be thankful and to show gratitude. Russ realised that he wouldn't be alive today without the random detection of his cancer, so he wanted to thank someone or the universe immediately. But as an atheist, he had no one to thank. If our lives are random sets of bones, tissues, gelatinous membranes, neurons, electrical impulses and chemicals, then who do we thank? Where do love and thanksgiving come from? Who do we direct them to? If we live or die without purpose, then what happens when we are given more time?

As Christians, we believe that all of our days are numbered and written in God's book before a single one comes to be. We believe that God holds all of our days in his hands. In response, we thank God regularly for his sovereign care and concern and for his redeeming actions towards us. For Russ, even with his atheist background, he had an intuitive sense that he needed to thank Someone – Someone who was in charge of his days. And he did.

I find it interesting that in closing, Russ longed to encourage people to have the tough conversations with God early on, while they still have breath. That's good advice! But I also think that we can't skip the comments Russ made prior to coming to faith in Jesus. In his 30s, he looked around and saw a lot of hypocrites in the church. He also saw denominations throwing rocks at each other. Let's pause quietly and consider whether we've had rocks in our hands lately, even small ones. There is so much that divides us, but we all need to remember daily that the church is the body of Christ worldwide, and that we have precious unity in our shared faith in Jesus. That unity is very precious to God! We have many differences of opinion, which we can acknowledge, but more than that, our unity is precious. We know it's precious because in the last moments before Jesus was arrested in the garden, his final fervent prayer was for unity in the church – that through our unity, 'the world may believe that you have sent me' (John 17:21). Jesus longed to protect our unity because he knew it would reveal God's wonderful glory to a watching world. Two thousand years later, we still need this prayer, desperately. Amazingly, God is still longing to answer it.

§

Perhaps you've noticed that most of the faith stories I have shared in this book so far have been from people who have come to faith in Jesus as adults. Some of them had a church-going background or Christian upbringing, but they made personal, life-changing responses to Jesus in their late teens and adulthood. Of course, I also spoke with a great many people who told me that they grew up always knowing and trusting Jesus from their earliest memories. Of the 300 people I interviewed, about 53 of them, or 18%, said that their faith in Jesus began in childhood. Their families and wider circles covered them in the love of Jesus and the awareness of God's presence. They said that over time, their faith in Jesus deepened, but in essence, they had always known him. A few of them seemed apologetic while describing their faith story to me, admitting it wasn't very exciting, perhaps even boring.

Every time, I said, 'No! Your story is not boring in the slightest. To have faith in Jesus from childhood is the most wonderful gift. Imagine being granted the knowledge of God and his goodness from your earliest memory. Imagine being held by God all these years. Imagine knowing Jesus' presence in such a precious, habit-forming way from childhood! How wonderful!'

Of all the people who told me about their faith as children, some had no recollection of a moment of decision or specific response to Jesus. They said they had *always* known and trusted Jesus. Others could remember a particular prayer, perhaps at age four, seven or 10, amidst a life of growing in faith in Jesus. **Christine** is a lovely example of that kind of story, remembering a particular moment at age seven.

6. Beautiful exceptions

'I came to faith in Jesus at the kitchen sink. My parents were OMF [Overseas Missionary Fellowship] missionaries in Taiwan, and I lived in Asia till I was 17. When I was five, I went to boarding school in Malaysia, and I did all of my primary school there. Then I went to high school in the Philippines.

After every four months in Malaysia, I would come home to my parents in Taiwan. I would always be angelically good for the first two weeks because I wanted to please them. Then my behaviour would slowly deteriorate. One night, I was back in Taiwan (during the deteriorating phase) and doing the dishes with Mum.

She said to me, "Does your heart sometimes feel a bit like this dirty plate?"

I nodded miserably and said yes. Then she put the plate in the water, and she washed it clean. She pulled it out of the water, and she said, "You know, Jesus can make your heart clean."

I literally became a Christian right there, at the kitchen sink. I was seven years old. I was young, but it was the moment God used. For me, it was the concept of forgiveness. Prior to that, I had begun to wonder at school, perhaps due to an excellent teacher who loved us and taught the Bible well. A few years later, at age 11, I fully acknowledged Jesus as Lord.

But my testimony always felt ordinary. As a teenager, I'd hear glamorous testimonies of other people coming to faith … and I'd feel mine wasn't very dramatic. It was so ordinary. I was almost embarrassed.

But also, from a very young age, I wanted to be a missionary. I was surrounded by missionaries – staff at the school, parents, kids. Perhaps I didn't know there was anything else you could be. So, I pushed myself to do things that were hard – praying out loud or doing a Bible reading. I knew it would help me prepare. And I've seen that as you strengthen your obedience muscle, God enables. He helps you to serve him.

I never imagined, though, as a teenager, where God would lead me. I ended up serving with OMF in southern Taiwan for 22 years. I was a church planter, but it was also very ordinary, not glamorous at all. I lived in a small town, in the south, that no one had ever heard of. It wasn't an important place. I spent a lot of time simply going out to the market, talking to people … the vegetable sellers and the small business owners. For all those years, I drank tea with people and chatted with them. I sought to care for them in their daily struggles. And all the time, I told them Bible stories. It was very ordinary. In 22 years, we saw very little fruit. Maybe two people came to faith in Jesus each year. But I have to trust that it's in God's timing. He's the one who opens their hearts. And he allows you to be there at the right time, sharing about Jesus.

It took me a long time, but I'm grateful now for my ordinary testimony. I've realised that it's been a long, steady process of getting to know Jesus better. And I've learned, more and more, that it's not about me; it's about who God is. I'm back in Australia now, which is a challenge after 22 years in Taiwan. It was such a big part of my identity. But it's the same here in Australia. I have to trust that God has me here. God is still

> at work here, and the people still need to hear about Jesus. So, I'm getting involved in all the ordinary things again. I've recently joined a birdwatching club, and I'm meeting people on the streets of Sydney, looking for opportunities to tell them about Jesus and the greatest story of them all.'

I love Christine's story. Of course, as she now agrees, it's not ordinary at all. It's beautiful, miraculous and unique, which is why I am including it in this chapter. God was at work in her heart throughout her life, including at boarding school and in all the seemingly ordinary moments at home. I appreciate how Christine's mum shared the message of forgiveness with her at the kitchen sink. I want to be more like her mum, noticing moments like that! And I thank God for Christian families and kitchen sinks and all the ways he works in us through ordinary, mundane moments that don't sound glamorous at all.

I also admire how Christine was open to serving God from an early age, leading her to serve in southern Taiwan with OMF for 22 years. We're going to discuss service and pouring out our gifts as a response to the gospel more fully in chapter 8, but for now, Christine's story is an encouragement to me. Some of us might read the words 'church planting in southern Taiwan' and think it sounds exciting. Christine told me, refreshingly, that it was ordinary. It involved going to the markets, drinking tea and doing all the normal things that she now continues to do back in Australia, except that it's now birdwatching and drinking tea. The key aspect is Christine's heart. Wherever she is, she longs to tell people the best story of all – the story we all need to hear. I thank God for Christine's willingness and honesty. And I pray that we would be encouraged in the same direction, continuing to strengthen our obedience muscles. As Christine says, as we do that, God enables. *Lord, we thank you for this reminder, and we ask you to help us serve you, love you and point to you, wherever we are.*

§

The majority of people who told me they came to faith in Jesus as children also told me they grew up in Christian families. They slowly absorbed God's truth through Sunday school, reading the Bible with their families and being constantly surrounded by the truth that Jesus was present, and they could pray to him. In contrast, a small number of people told me they came to a genuine faith in Jesus as children without that background at all. Some of them, like me, heard the gospel through school friends and contacts who were Christians. **Caroline**, on the other hand, said she went to Sunday school for six months at age four, and then after that, she had no contact with Christians for decades. But she always knew that Jesus was real, and she believed in him.

> 'I grew up on a dairy farm in Gympie. My mother often told me I was ugly and unlovable. She had six children, and one of them (my younger brother) was from an extramarital affair. Whenever he did anything wrong, I would be blamed, and my father would belt me with the poly pipe. Some years later, my mother turned to witchcraft.
>
> At age four, we were sent to Sunday school. I was too young to read, but I was given a notebook with stickers and Bible verses in it. One of the verses said that Jesus loved the little children. Since then, I've always known it, deep inside me. God loves me.

But we only went to Sunday school for six months. After that, I didn't meet any other Christians, or go to church, for decades. My home life was very hard. From age seven, I worked on the farm before school, and for two hours after school. We had over 120 cows, and I milked them morning and night, every day. At school, I also felt isolated because I was always working on the farm. I wasn't allowed to go on camps or join in with the others.

But in high school, I was given a Gideons New Testament and I read it. It didn't make much sense to me, except for John 3:16, "For God so loved the world that he gave his one and only Son, that whoever believes in him shall not perish but have eternal life."

I knew that God loved me. I knew that Jesus died for me and that God was with me. But I also ignored Jesus for many years. After school, I met my future husband, and I trained as a nurse. Nursing is very science-based, but I saw many things at the hospital, even miracles, that didn't fit with science. I noticed that when people died with a faith in God, there was a peace. For others, they would sometimes die in terror, or as if they were fighting for every breath. It was very noticeable, and it made me wonder.

One night, I was going to see a patient and I heard an audible voice from God, warning me of something in the patient's condition. After that, I started to open my Bible more regularly. How do I get to know you, God?

I still didn't know any Christians, and I'd never been to church. My husband was the same. We had our first son, and our second six years later. But three months after our second son was born, he was asleep and I heard the same audible voice from God, "Go and get the baby."

I went to his cot, and he was cold and grey. I went into resus mode, and he started to breathe again. For the next year, he had many episodes of central sleep apnoea. It was silent and deadly. We had alarms. Sometimes, he would set them off 10 to 12 times a night. I found myself praying all the time. "God, you've got him – you can save him." I didn't know very much back then, but I prayed all the time, because I knew that life and breath come from God.

Eighteen months later, our daughter was born, and she had the same condition. I was praying again – the Lord's Prayer, in the shower every night, along with buckets of tears. "Please God, get us through the night. Give us strength and wisdom." That's when I really learnt to walk with God. He was always present. Afterwards, we got the children baptised to say thank you.

We went to a church for the first time ever! The minister followed us up and visited us. He said the church was doing the Alpha (evangelistic) course. We had three kids at the time, so we couldn't go, but they said they could meet at our house. They did that, and then that group turned into a Bible study group … which lasted for the next 10 years.

I've seen that God is good all the time. Hard things happen, but he's got us, he's carrying us. He loves us. That's why Jesus

> came. Sometimes I want to transplant the love of God I feel in my heart and give it to others, so that they too can be assured of God's deep, deep love for them.'

I find Caroline's story amazing. Despite having such little Christian input, she always knew that God was real and that he loved her. She held onto that truth through her difficult upbringing and decades of busy work and family life. Although she admits she ignored Jesus for a while, she remained open to his truth. During that time, she received a Gideons New Testament, saw evidence of peace in her believing patients as they died and heard God speak to her audibly, both at work and at home. She longed to know him more and experienced his presence and enabling while struggling with serious illness in her children. Finally, she went to church to have her children baptised because she wanted to say thank you. From that point on, she grew in her faith and understanding of Jesus.

It's interesting that the thanksgiving aspect of Caroline's journey is similar to Russ's story – the same need to thank a God who is present and at work in our lives for good. I also love the fact that Caroline prayed the Lord's Prayer constantly during her years of fear and stress. She didn't know much back then, but she knew she could pray and that God was with her. That's the very best truth that any of us can know. Often, in times of stress, our more intellectual or complex thoughts about God go out the window. We tend to repeat short, favourite psalms, sing Sunday school songs like 'Jesus Loves Me, This I Know' or repeat the Lord's Prayer, like Caroline, over and over again, letting the words seep into our adrenaline-fuelled bodies. 'Our Father in heaven, hallowed be your name, your kingdom come, your will be done, on earth as it is in heaven' (Matt 6:9–10). And God hears us, giving us his beautiful comfort and peace beyond our imaginations. May Caroline's story also provide the prompts we need today, especially for those of us under severe stress.

§

I could go on and on, adding more faith stories as beautiful, unique accounts of God at work in our lives. But I'm going to finish this chapter with a story from our friend **Shaun**. He described his unbelieving, questioning background and then the unexpected work of God in providing the answers he needed.

> 'I've always been a science-based person. I'm wired that way. My whole career has been based on logic and analysis – how things are created and built. It started in high school and then continued at university – I got degrees that covered engineering, human physiology, physics and chemistry.
>
> After university, my girlfriend and I moved out together. Everything was fine. Then Tracey became a Christian. It felt very sudden to me. She started saying that Jesus was the answer. What was the question? She'd been talking with some girls at her work who gave her books to read, including the Bible.
>
> I had a Roman Catholic background, and my mum had even sent me to an Anglican Sunday school, but I hated it. I thought it was all gobbledegook. As the years passed, my main issue was with creation versus evolution. At university, the lecturers were constantly talking about cells that turned into fish, then

frogs, then land-based animals. There was no other way to view it. The idea of a Creator was all bunkum to me, equating with a fairy story.

But Tracey kept talking to me about Jesus. And along the way, our relationship changed. According to her, God had a bigger plan. She asked me to go to church with her and I agreed ... because I loved her. She also gave me a Bible, and I read it for five seconds and threw it on the bed. It was still bunkum. But I went to church with her four times in a row. I sat up the back.

On the way there, though, each week, I had questions. Tracey replied, "Let's see what the pastor says."

Then, every week, we sat in church, and the pastor answered my exact questions in the sermon. He looked me straight in the eye, and he spoke with his booming voice about the exact thing I was thinking about.

I said to Tracey, "What's going on? Did you talk to this guy?"

She said, "No." She didn't.

After four weeks, I said to her, "Yeah, okay. There might be something here."

The minister then lent me a whole pile of videos from scientists on the topics of design and creation and evolution. I binge-watched them for six hours in a row. They were similar in style to John Lennox ... and enough to raise questions in me. It turned out there could be a different, scientific way to observe and interpret the world around us. Take cells, for example. They do these amazing things; they reproduce, in order, in perfect design. Or look at the Moon and the tides. The water moves in and out in cycles, which influences the ecosystem. There are so many "accidents" that work absolutely perfectly on so many levels. Could they be random?

I started to wonder. Was it possible that there was a Creator? It would mean I wasn't in control, and that I was a creation. It threw me into confusion and challenged everything I thought. If I wasn't at the top of the pile ... if I was created, then I had a problem. It meant that I was in a different position, in front of a Creator.

I sat on my bed and didn't know what to do. My position had changed. I said, "God, if you are who I think you are, help me to believe."

The next morning, I just knew it was true. There was a Creator. Something changed in me, overnight, and I believed. "In the beginning was the Word, and the Word was with God, and the Word was God" (John 1:1–3).

I suddenly knew who I was as a creation. Previously, my questions had been around Jesus – who he was and what he had done. It hadn't made any sense to me. But when my position changed overnight, I knew I needed Jesus. I owed a debt that I couldn't pay. But Jesus had made me right with the Creator, and I needed to respond.

Overnight, it changed the way I thought and acted. I know God did it inside me. I could never have changed myself. All my life I had been a person who loved being in control, and then that day I trusted God, who was in control. It wasn't bunkum at all!'

It's such a wonderful reminder, isn't it? Our Creator God is aware of our repeated questions and highly sceptical attitudes. He knows our hearts and provides his answers in his timing. As he does so, he points us back to something far more marvellous than dividing cells. He shows us *himself*, the designer of the dividing cells and the maker of the Moon, the tides and the water cycles. I love the miraculous aspect of Shaun's story. He agreed to go to church with Tracey four times in a row, but on the way to church, he had specific questions in his mind. The preacher answered those *exact* questions in his sermon, without knowing it.

Shaun also told me that at the time, that particular church in western Sydney was very small. It held half-a-dozen elderly people, along with Tracey and Shaun sitting up the back. And yet God used that tiny church and the faithful pastor, with his booming voice, as well as the videos on creation that Shaun watched later. Then there was the moment of sacred revelation. Shaun just *knew* it was true, which is perhaps even more amazing given that he was such a scientifically wired soul. He couldn't explain it, but he knew he was a creation in front of his Creator God and that he needed Jesus. I love hearing stories like this!

It makes me more expectant. If God can repeatedly reveal himself to sceptics like Shaun and Russ, or to angry, disillusioned people like Norm and Chris, or to tiny children like Christine and Caroline, then he can reveal himself to us and our family members today. He can capture our hearts and the hearts of those we love, convincing us of his powerful truth and answers in Christ. May that be the case today.

7
New wineskins

In every faith journey, God continues to grow us, often over decades. He reveals himself to us in Christ, and then he continues to teach us profound new truths about his grace as we journey with Christ for decades. This is what we need! The initial moments when we acknowledge his Lordship are amazing and life-changing, but they are not the end. God compels us more and more by his Spirit and his Word as we submit to Jesus. Sometimes the journey is extremely convoluted, or it includes seeming dead ends and obstacles, but nevertheless, God is always shaping our inner beings and forming brand-new habits and desires in us. At times, the change is immediate and obvious. At other times, the change is very slow or brought about by circumstances we would never choose.

Looking back over my life, it feels like the times of most growth in my walk with Jesus have also been the times when much growth was required. I learned about God as my true source of patience and contentment while I was living and homeschooling in a Himalayan village without running water or electricity. I learned about God's deep comfort and care while weeping over five pregnancy losses. I learned about Jesus as my true source of peace while sitting in a hospital waiting room as Darren underwent extended surgery for a life-threatening heart condition. Even as I write this paragraph in short sentences, I realise I can make it sound easy. It wasn't at all. The deepest lessons that God has brought about in my heart have been slow and arduous, as they still are today, on that shared journey as we each attempt to let God conform us more and more into his likeness.

I'm sure you can also look back on your own life and see the same patterns of God as he has taught, led and grown you, often through unexpected and painful times, as well as smoother pathways. In each case, as I talked to 300 people about their faith journeys, they all inevitably told me about the slow work of God in their hearts over time, *after* their initial trust in Jesus. Often, that slow work was the main story.

We know that in Matthew 9:14, some of John's disciples came to Jesus to ask why his disciples didn't fast. Jesus explained to them about the new life and the old life. He said, 'No one sews a patch of unshrunk cloth on an old garment, for the patch will pull away from the garment, making the tear worse. Neither do people pour new wine into old wineskins. If they do, the skins will burst; the wine will run out, and the wineskins will be ruined. No, they pour new wine into new wineskins, and both will be preserved' (Matt 9:16–17).

In that question to Jesus, John's disciples were referring to the Old Testament law, or the expression of the law at the time by the Pharisees. Jesus' reply was beautiful. He said that following him involves an entirely new way of being, doing and trusting. It's a brand-new garment, a new wineskin. Our old habits and ways of thinking will be completely transformed by the Holy Spirit. We will be made brand new in our inner selves as the Spirit resides in our hearts and keeps shaping us. And that new life will be visibly evident outwardly in our behaviour, words and actions, more and more.

Some of the people who shared with me described that transformative process as being sudden and instantaneous, like Alan and his metaphor of walking into the Narnia cupboard. He said that his whole life changed. Others, of course, described the process as being very slow or convoluted, like Jeremy, who admitted that his life hasn't been a fairytale. But he clings to Jesus. I'd love to share a few more examples of that process as an encouragement. We will begin with **Cameron**, whose life was transformed by God, unexpectedly, in prison.

'Before 2004, I'd never even had a speeding fine. Then, in my late 20s, I was an acting general manager of a finance corporation. I made an investment on behalf of the company, and I received a financial kickback … which I should have known was the wrong thing to do. I went to court, and I was sentenced to jail for two-and-a-half years. It was horrible – for myself, for my wife, for our kids. At the time, my wife was heavily pregnant with our third child. It was atrocious.

I remember that in the trial the barrister asked me if I thought what I did was dishonest. I said, "Yes." That pretty much threw our case out the window. But it also meant that, for the first time, I owned up to what I did instead of blaming everyone else.

Before going to jail, I probably thought that being a Christian was about being a good person and following the rules. In jail, though, my faith became very real for me, much more than before. I read the Bible, and for the first time, I wanted to see what it really said about Jesus and salvation. I wanted to live it.

7. New wineskins

At first, it was really hard. I thought that God had forgotten about me. He knew I was sorry. He knew I didn't mean it. Why didn't he rescue me from this?

But then, it slowly changed. I found myself thrust into a community of people who were the kingpins of the illegal lifestyle. All my biases were laid aside. They were just blokes. They had been dealt hard stuff. Some of them had never had a visitor in 20 years. And here was I, with an opportunity to share that God loves them, despite what they'd done, despite what they'd become. It was an amazing opportunity. I had inmates coming to my room, all the time, asking me to pray for them. And I did. We talked about what it meant to have a right relationship with God. I saw so much change in them over the years.

In Matthew 9:12, Jesus said, "It is not the healthy who need a doctor, but those who are ill." It's true. Jesus was sent to the world for the sick. Sometimes, people on the outside find it hard to accept that there's anything wrong with them. But the unhealthy, or the people on the inside, they know they're bad dudes. They know they need help and forgiveness. In some ways, it makes it easier to say, "Despite that, God loves you." They were willing to accept it. It was so different to what they thought Christianity was about!

I know I'm different now. My wife and kids are different. We're stronger in a lot of ways. I started doing Bible college in jail, and after I got out, I went into ministry with young people – in churches and now as a school chaplain. Before that time, I would have thought that getting a good job, a good house, and the kids in good schools were the important things.

> And whilst they are fine things, they're not the most important things. These days, my wife and I sometimes say to each other that we wish there'd been an easier way to learn those deep lessons about God's grace and what's important – but in the end, we're thankful for it. We know that the true gospel message gives lasting hope.'

In a million years, Cameron would never have chosen time in prison to learn deep lessons of God's grace. Yet, somehow, God allowed it and worked through it, changing Cameron's heart forever. I find Cameron's story very humbling, reminding me that we are all unwell and in need of salvation. There is deep beauty in a broken, honest, repentant heart. Even in the worst circumstances, there are opportunities not only to receive grace but to also show grace to others.

I also relate to Cameron's statement that people 'on the inside' know they're bad dudes. They know they need help and forgiveness. Perhaps it's the extreme example of an unravelled life – the absolute end of a rope, the end of pretence, the end of blame and the end of superficial hope. In prison, outward circumstances can force a person to face up to their own unravelling and admit they need help. Having visited a number of prisons myself, I've gone away each time feeling humbled, knowing that I've been taught a great deal by the people living there, especially in regard to admitting need. For Cameron, he was one of them. He lived with them, prayed with them and shared God's love with them. Indeed, there was no more 'us and them' at all.

Cameron's story challenges my pride, my stereotypes and my tendency to categorise people. It invites me to pray humbly and look around me in fresh ways. It compels me to see God's upside-down mercy and grace in my own life – an invitation needed by all of us, wherever we are. It also compels me to question: Am I healthy? Is anyone healthy? Or are we all unwell and in desperate need of a gracious invitation from God? Jesus' words in Matthew's Gospel remind us to never forget our own naked state or to sit in judgement of others. *Lord, we ask today that your healing power would touch our hearts in fresh ways, in all the ways we need.*

§

On the topic of wellness, or the lack of it, and our response, here is **Anthea**'s story. She's a dear friend of mine who has lived with chronic, incurable pain for many years. She speaks profoundly about tears.

> 'I've had severe, chronic pain for the last 13 years. It's caused by a combination of health conditions, and it affects my whole body. It's relentless … and impossible to escape – every day and every night the pain is there. Sometimes I can't leave the house, or even leave my bed. I can't even describe it to you. It feels like there's no part of my life that the pain hasn't impacted – all my daily activities, work, social life, church, finances, relationships … everything. It makes doing even the simplest of tasks a huge challenge. Some days tying my shoelaces or making a phone call can end up feeling like a hard-won victory.
>
> But for a while now, I've been thinking about tears. Psalm 126:5 says, "Those who sow with tears will reap with songs of joy." I've cried so many tears! But what does it mean for me to sow in tears? I've been pondering it for years. It tells me firstly that it's okay to have tears. God somehow expects tears, and he collects them in a bottle (Ps 56:8). I often think that God better

have a really big bottle, in my case! But we also know that Jesus wept when Lazarus died (John 11:35). Jesus grieved over his friend. That tells me it's okay to weep and grieve.

Maybe we have three options. On the one hand, we could try and squash our tears or prevent them from coming out. That wouldn't work very well in my case! Or, alternatively, we could let our tears be the master of us. That's not great either. It can lead to despair.

But there is a third way. God says that we can cry our tears out to him, and he hears us. Lately, I've been picturing all my tears falling onto a parched land. They drop onto dry, cracked soil, one by one, but over time, growth comes, maybe a tiny plant. When I offer my tears to God, he takes them and uses them. I don't know what the little plant will be yet. But God promises me that my tears won't be wasted. They might even be like rain and refreshment for someone else.

And there is a promise at the end of Revelation that I hold on to. When Jesus returns and restores everything, God will tenderly wipe away every tear from our eyes (Rev 21:4). Won't that be beautiful?'

It will indeed be beautiful. When Jesus returns and restores everything, God will tenderly wipe away all the tears we've ever cried. He will heal all our sicknesses and diseases. He will remove all our pain and burdens. We will be able to get out of bed, tie our shoelaces and run outside.

For me, I've been appreciating Anthea's honest reflections on her faith journey for many years now, and I love her imagery of a garden.

7. New wineskins

Whenever I think of it, I imagine bare soil in mine, perhaps with scattered plants in need of nurture, and some weeds. But then I picture the tears that I've cried recently or over many years, spilling over and falling onto that garden, onto the tender shoots and dry ground, sometimes softly and quietly, and at other times with great groaning and emotion. Anthea is so right. There is a gift in tears. They can bring healing and release. They can tell our stories of pain, longing and joy. They can express the emotions that we need to release in safe places. They can bring connection to each other and to God. Indeed, they can bring us back to our God, who always hears us and knows our tears, even the silent, secret ones. One day, he will wipe them away very tenderly.

Anthea's story also compels me to pray, not only for her and others in ongoing chronic pain, but for all those of us who continue to carry burdens. May God, in his tenderness, take our tears and use them for good and for his glory. May he also give us rest and refreshment in his time, that we might sing songs of joy in knowing him, as Psalm 126 describes so well.

§

Sometimes the lessons of God's care or sufficiency are burned into our souls over very long periods of time, as is the case with Anthea. At other times, the lessons arrive in a mad, all-consuming rush. I'd love you to meet our friend **Cecily**.

> 'I was always terrified by the thought of bushfires. I grew up in South Africa, where we didn't have bushfires, so it was a new thing when we moved to Australia. We bought a house in the Blue Mountains, with bush on two sides of the house. The real

estate agent cheerfully pointed at the valley, and he said, "If a fire comes, it will come from down there …"

Years went by. Some summers were better than others, although I was always nervous. Then, on Boxing Day 2001, my husband was pottering around outside. He saw a small spot fire in the bush, and he tried to put it out. Next minute, he saw a wall of flame coming towards us and the house. I was inside, putting the kettle on for a cup of tea. He rushed inside and I looked out the laundry window. The door started smouldering. There was no time to get out. I thought, "Right, that's it … our house is on fire."

I closed all the internal doors, and I could hear the windows shattering. Our daughter and son-in-law were also with us, and they started pulling down the curtains from the windows. There was fire between us and the car. The phone rang in the middle of it. My husband answered it and he said, "I'm sorry, I can't talk right now; the house is on fire." Meanwhile, I was on the floor, praying like mad, as you can imagine, asking the Lord for mercy.

The fire started coming through the internal doors. I said, "We've got to get out!" We grabbed the dog, and we all scarpered out the front door. The back part of our daughter's car had already melted. We got in ours and we drove up the street, through thick smoke. By then, our whole house was in flames. We were totally amazed that we were alive. We could so easily have died. Maybe that made a difference to our attitude afterwards.

> The next day, the reporters came to our street, and they filmed us. I said that it was all right with us. I said that we love the Lord, and we know that we are loved by him. We had lost everything we owned, but we were so thankful to be alive.
>
> There were a couple of Bible verses that I kept quoting to myself. One very meaningful line (that I also shared with the governor-general when he came to visit our street!) was the second half of Jesus' words in Luke 12:15: "Watch out! Be on your guard against all kinds of greed; life does not consist in an abundance of possessions."
>
> How true that is. Life does not consist in an abundance of possessions. Losing everything we owned has made us more generous. We were absolutely stunned by the outpouring of generosity towards us, afterwards. It made us realise that everything we have is a gift from God and we are to hold it lightly. We can enjoy our possessions, but we can use everything we have for God. We don't need to hoard anything. And we know that God is good all of the time. His plans are always good. I remember saying to someone, at the time, "Well, I'm not taking my possessions with me when I die, so I just said goodbye to them a bit earlier than I thought …"¹

It's a hair-raising and remarkable story, especially when told in Cecily's South African accent with her dry sense of humour. I can also imagine her husband, Lance, answering the phone in the middle of the fire and apologising that he was a bit too busy to talk! But they both escaped the house and drove down the street as it burnt down behind them with all their possessions inside. All they had left were the clothes on their backs.

I remember talking to both Cecily and Lance at our local church soon after the event. They were so thankful to be alive and for God's provision through generous friends. But it was also a hard, ongoing lesson about riches. Cecily's story is a reminder of God's calling to put our wealth and possessions in their rightful position. We are not ruled by them. We are not taking them with us. We are not what we own. We are not defined by them. We are not in control. But perhaps it can be hard sometimes to know our own hearts. Are we relying on our possessions, or finding undue comfort in them, even a tiny bit?

It can be hard to know, and of course, the true litmus test is the one we would never choose – losing everything in a moment, like Cecily and Lance. What would we do or say if it were us? For them, God granted a fresh perspective on possessions and generosity, which has continued to change them over the years since then as they have rebuilt their home. I remember the day I was chatting to them at church, and they told me that they used to collect musical instruments, amongst other things, before the fire. They had stored up a beautiful collection. But now, if they're ever tempted to hoard anything or store up possessions for themselves, they look at each other and say the one word: 'Barns.' May we also be granted a fresh perspective on the things we own today. *Lord, please help us to remember that everything we have is a gift from you. Help us to relax our grip and hold those things lightly.*

§

As followers of Jesus, every aspect of our lives is made brand new by the Holy Spirit – our attitudes towards our work, ministry, freedom, tears, riches and also our relationships with God and each other. A

7. New wineskins

few years ago, I met **Michael** while I was staying in Tennant Creek, Northern Territory. I was very moved by his words about relationships.

> 'I live in Tennant Creek now, in the Northern Territory. I moved here in 1978, and I got a job working for the town council. Later I went up to Darwin to study at Bible college and to find out how God wants his people to live. I became a believer in Jesus a long time before that. I've been going to the church that meets here in Tennant Creek, in the Australian Indigenous Ministries building on the corner of Standley Street, since 1985. We have Sunday services, and we have gatherings through the week.
>
> In Aboriginal culture, skins are really important. It's a system that tells us who we can marry and who we can't marry. In some groups, though, if someone is from the wrong skin, you can't look that person in the eye, or you can't say their name out loud, or share any room or space with them. It can cause trouble at times. If someone from the wrong skin walks into a building, someone else may walk out.
>
> But in our church here in Tennant Creek, there are no skin customs like that. We do follow good traditional ways, like we respect our elders, but we don't avoid people. That's what Christ has done for us. He's made us one family, so there's none of that here. We have unity in Christ, and that means it doesn't matter about our tribe, or our family disputes; we're all one in Christ here. We still marry according to our customs, and we follow other cultural traditions that are good, but we don't do it if it's contrary to the gospel. We show love to each other, because we know we've been loved.

> Of course, we still have our problems. But when I first heard the gospel, I couldn't believe that God loved me. He loved me. In Romans 5 it says that Jesus died for us while we were sinners. And we're all sinners. We're not perfect. We have troubles. But God loves us. That's what it says in Romans 5.'

Isn't that wonderful? Michael and his fellow believers follow their traditional Indigenous ways and customs in every positive aspect, but their unity in Christ is at another level altogether. It completely transforms their relationships. They know they are one in Christ, and so they show love to each other because they have been loved.

I think we all need this reminder, and it fits so well with Paul's letter to the Romans. Paul was very careful with his use of pronouns in chapter 5. He said that God demonstrates his own love for *us*. While *we* were still sinners, Christ died for *us*. It was plural, not individual. It was the body of Christ, bound together by our belief in Christ. We are not a fragile mix of single units. I recall what Michael described to me in Tennant Creek. In their church, he said, they are united as one family. They are united in Christ because Christ has brought them together, and therefore, there is no one who is unwanted, left out or avoided. There is no one who would walk out of a room if someone else walked in.

This is a challenge for all of us! May we all continue to remember that the gospel unites us, binding us together in new families with people we might normally avoid or ignore. *Lord, we thank you for this needed reminder, and we ask again that our unity in Christ would be wonderfully evident in our communities today.*

§

7. New wineskins

A large part of our ordinary days and years is spent in the realm of paid work, in all of its different guises. Naturally, in chatting with people, many of them told me about how God had led them at work or how their faith worked out in practise at work. Although each story was unique and different, the concept of success was common to all of them. Meet **Jo**, who is a work colleague of my husband, Darren, and a fellow believer.

> 'I work in academia. It can be highly competitive. This is my eighth year. For me, being excellent in science is part of my worship of God. But it can be difficult to achieve excellence. Success in science often means having significant impact and influence through a research profile, publications, grants and other achievements. As scientists, we build knowledge by asking important questions and testing new ideas, but these do not always work out. It often seems that the impact of my work falls short of what success looks like. And I'm often reminded of how I have failed to achieve. For example, the university faculty sends out regular emails, rightly congratulating various staff on their achievements. I received a few such emails this past week. Reading them reminded me of my inadequacy. Have I failed to honour God because my life has not looked as successful as I thought it should have? Will I ever be good enough?
>
> I have been reading through Hebrews, though, and meditating on 12:1–2. We are called to "run with perseverance the race marked out for us, fixing our eyes on Jesus, the pioneer and perfector of faith."

> It is so easy to lose sight of what's important – like Peter, seeing only the waves when he tried to walk to Jesus on water. But we are to set our sights on Christ, who for the joy set before him endured the cross. He entered into our pain, and he endured for us. He understands.
>
> What does success mean to God? The day after reading the faculty emails, I read Hebrews during my morning quiet time, and I was reminded that success means to know God in Jesus Christ and enjoy him, to love him and to love our fellow man. When faced with inadequacy and despair, I am reminded to fix my eyes on Christ, to have faith and courage, to keep going in his great strength, and to finish the race.'

Perhaps Jo's faith story seems familiar to many of us. It's the regular challenge to fix our eyes on Jesus in our places of work amidst emails, deadlines, business meetings and the somewhat unwelcome feeling that we haven't met even our own expectations of ourselves, let alone anyone else's. Paid work seems to amplify all those feelings while also absorbing so many hours of our days!

I appreciated Jo's reminder to read Hebrews. It's clear that in God's eyes, success means to know him in Christ. It means to enjoy him, love him and love our fellow humans, always fixing our eyes on Jesus. This can be especially hard whenever there is the clamour of other loud, demanding voices. Perhaps we need to pause again and remember. May the Lord remind us today that he understands, he walked our walk and he knows more than we can imagine about unmet expectations. *Lord, we pray today that we would fix our eyes on you during our work hours and every other hour of the day. Show us again that you are truly the author and perfector of our faith.*

7. New wineskins

§

We all want to fix our eyes on Jesus. We pray for the energy to do so more and more at work, at home and in every part of life. Sometimes, we pray for protection, healing or opportunities, and God miraculously provides. At other times, we don't see answers at all. It's at those times that God often does a deeper work in our hearts, teaching us about himself and his sufficiency. That has been the case for **Steph**.

> 'I feel like God has been teaching me the same thing over and over again. God is good, and he is in control. And I am not.
>
> In 2011, my husband and I moved to the Tiwi Islands. We were working at a school run by Indigenous Australian elders.
>
> During that time, we started trying to have kids. It was really hard. Years went by. It was a real challenge to my faith. Some of the other Christians in the community were saying things like, "You just need to have more faith. You need to trust God more. If you have faith, he will answer."
>
> I really struggled for a long time. I started to believe maybe it was my fault, or that I didn't have enough faith. Then one day, a friend on Instagram shared a quote: "… and if not, he is still good." I picked up my Bible and found the story of Shadrach, Meshach and Abednego. When they were thrown into the furnace, they said to King Nebuchadnezzar that "the God we serve is able to deliver us from it … But even if he does not … we will not serve your gods or worship the image of gold you have set up" (Dan 3:17–18).

It meant a lot to me. God was able to rescue them, but even if he didn't, they would still trust him. He would still be good. It gave me a lot more confidence. God is good regardless of whether he gives us what we want or not. He's in control. It wasn't about my faith or lack of it. It's up to God. And if we couldn't have kids, it would be hard, but it would be okay. God would still be God.

In 2014, we met with an adoption agency. If we wanted to adopt, we would have to leave the Tiwi Islands. We gave ourselves a deadline. If we weren't pregnant by October of that year, we would go through the adoption process. Then I fell pregnant in September! We were really excited!

But for my whole pregnancy, I had severe perinatal anxiety. What if something happened to me or the baby? When our baby was three weeks old, I had mastitis. It turned septic in a matter of hours. I was well versed by my midwives on what to do if I got a fever with mastitis, so I dutifully went to the ED. I was in hospital for four days, and the doctors said I might not have made it if I hadn't come in. I was reminded again: I'm not in control. God is still God. Even if I had died, which was possible, God would still be good. It was scary, but I had a real sense that God was in control.

Two years later our second child was born, and when she was two weeks old, I got sepsis again. I remember being in emergency; all the bells started going off and the nurse yelled, "Sepsis!" I was rushed into the resuscitation area and then taken to the ICU [intensive care unit] to try to save my organs. I spent two days in the ICU and another eight days in hospital.

> Again, we were told that if we hadn't gone in, I wouldn't have lived. It was horrific and scary. We had to really practise what we already knew. There is so much heartache and suffering and pain in the world. We don't have much control. But God is in control. It feels like, over and over again, he's given me opportunities to learn that.'

It's a needed reminder, isn't it? In the biblical account of Daniel, the exiled Jews were told that if they didn't bow down before an image of gold, they would be thrown into a blazing furnace. Daniel's three friends were duly punished in that way, but prior to going in, they looked to Yahweh. They knew him. They said they were convinced. They knew he could rescue them but also that he might choose not to rescue them. Either way, they would still worship him.

I love the way Steph has been learning that profound lesson over many years, as God has been tenderly teaching her. God is always good, holy and unfathomable. He is able to do as he pleases, and he delights to save us. It's true for all of us. Whether or not his actions are the ones we would choose, we still want to worship him. We still want to trust his good purposes in everything. He is in control, but he is not always fathomable. We do experience fear and heartache on this earth. But God is still good, and we want to praise him today, in the middle of it, even in the bits we don't understand at all. *Lord, please remind us today that our hope is in you alone, amidst both joy and heartache and struggle. Show us your sufficiency again, we pray.*

§

There is another part of the journey with Christ that seems to take a very long time to learn, indeed, an entire lifetime. And that is understanding the Father heart of God and his deep, unshakeable grace towards us. Many people described a similar journey to me. They described it in different ways, using different phrases. They talked about different circumstances that brought about new depth in receiving God's love.

Our friend **Richard** described profound learning during a time of severe burnout following Christian ministry. Suddenly, he could no longer do anything useful for God.

> 'I grew up thinking that I was always in trouble with God. My image of God was that he was a bit scary ... and that I wasn't good enough. It distorted my view of God as "Father". I wasn't actually a naughty child. I was pretty good. But in the early 70s when I was only very small, everyone was watching the Left Behind video and singing, "I wish we'd all been ready ..." I was worried that I'd be left behind because I wasn't good enough. If I came home from school early and my mum wasn't there, I'd be worried that she'd been raptured. So, I would say the sinner's prayer every day (for years) just in case it hadn't worked before.
>
> For a long time, I thought I needed to work hard for God and earn my place. From the age of 24, I started working full-time for Christian organisations, both overseas and locally. I've been doing that ever since. But in 2011, I burnt out. It was really severe. I was working 60-plus hours a week, and it was a stressful job with lots of responsibility. I hit the wall. I couldn't get out of bed for six months. The doctor said I had depression and anxiety. It was very hard.

But there's something about pain and suffering that God uses to grow us. There's an opportunity, in the middle of a crisis, to actually do some business with God. I think we often try to avoid pain at all costs, but God will bring growth about, in his way. For me, I started seeing a Christian psychologist, as well as doing a spiritual formation course at Bible college, and I went to a healing ministry. The burnout stripped me of everything I thought I was ... and I actually surrendered to God.

But the God who I surrendered to was a loving Father. I wasn't in trouble. I realised for the first time that I was a child of God. Even though I was in burnout, I wasn't in trouble. God delighted in me. It was amazing. I realised my identity was as a child of God who was beloved. There was a real gentleness there. And because of Christ's work on the cross, I was now seen by God as his child. I was in Christ, robed in the righteousness of Christ ...

I could call God "Abba, Father"! It changed my life. It's such an intimate term; it's a primal cry from the heart. It's so personal.

After the burnout, I was worried that I would never get a job in Christian ministry again. But I remember going for my next job interview. The interviewer nodded, and he said, "Good! And what did God teach you during the burnout?"

I realised then that my relationship with God wasn't about work performance. It was about my whole identity as who God says I am. And I am his beloved child.'

It's an honest, profound story, isn't it? The God to whom Richard surrendered is a loving Father. Richard wasn't in trouble. He was loved. He could cry, 'Abba, Father' – the primal cry from his heart. Having known Richard for over 20 years, I have definitely seen these ongoing, softening changes in him. It hasn't been merely words. It has been God at work in his heart, evidenced in all of his life and attitudes.

Richard's story also makes me reflect on my own attitudes to God and wonder if there have been times in my own life when I've subconsciously thought I needed to work harder for God or that I wasn't doing enough.

I love the truth found in Romans 8:15. The Spirit we received brought about our adoption. We can cry 'Abba, Father'. Even when we can't get out of bed or do anything useful at all, we are his beloved children. Our identity is in him. We have been adopted by grace, and that's enough.

I also appreciate Richard's reminder that in times of crisis, there may be an opportunity for us to do some business with God and allow him to do his necessary, softening work in us. As people who often try to shield ourselves from pain or run in the other direction, we can stop and ask God to help us turn to him in all things. *Lord, we thank you that you long to work in our hearts in the hardest times. Please help us to call you Abba, Father.*

§

As well as doing that deep, needed work in our hearts during times of crisis, God also works in our hearts in the more mundane, ordinary, yet still frustrating days. My friend **Elizabeth** has long been an encouragement to me in that regard.

'I have significant mental health issues … and I've always been very hard on myself, ever since I can remember. For example, if something didn't go right or the way I felt it should go, I would overreact emotionally. I would rage – at the thing that went wrong, or at myself for letting it go wrong. Even my daughter said she felt scared during those times. It's been a long road.

But I am noticing change, slowly. Last year, I started having a problem with my foot. I couldn't walk on it, and I needed foot reconstruction surgery – which meant that afterwards, I had to be off my foot for three months. I moved around the house on a mobility scooter. It was frustrating! But God used that time to slowly build me up in my faith.

I remember during that time, I was reading Ephesians, and I noticed the prayer in 1:17. Paul said, "I keep asking that the God of our Lord Jesus Christ, the glorious Father, may give you the Spirit of wisdom and revelation, so that you may know him better."

That's what God wants. And that's what I'm seeking this year – to know God better – to know who he is and how he is at work in my life.

I remember unpacking the dishwasher one day, during the time I couldn't walk – I was kneeling on my mobility scooter, and I accidentally knocked over the cat's feeding station. The whole thing went crashing to the floor, including the porcelain food bowls. There was china and cat food everywhere! I couldn't even get down on the floor to clean it up. But I turned around and I stayed calm. I had a look, I saw the mess, and I went back to unloading the dishwasher. I didn't rage!

> In that moment, I thanked God for the healing he is slowly bringing into my life. I know that I'm so vastly different to how I used to be. And whilst it's been slow, and at times unnoticeable, it's happened, and it continues to happen. So that's my ongoing prayer for this year. Lord, keep changing me so that I might know you better ...'

Isn't that wonderful? God is slowly changing Elizabeth's heart, including her tendency to overreact to frustrating situations. I see myself in Elizabeth's story! I am very encouraged by the fact that Elizabeth is deliberately looking back and seeing that she is changing. In this case, the mess covered the floor, but she stayed calm. In the past, she would have exploded. Not only did Elizabeth notice the profound changes in herself, but she also attributed them to God, whose Spirit is at work in her life.

For me, like Elizabeth, I find the prayer in Ephesians 1 very helpful. Paul was praying for the small Ephesian church, reminding them of God's vast, sweeping plans for the world in Christ. A key part of the prayer was that God would give them the Spirit of wisdom and revelation *so that they might know him better*. Amazingly, that's what God wants for us too. He desires that deep work in us more than an easy path, comfort, physical resources or even a productive ministry. He wants us to know him better. In his sovereignty, God might use challenges, frustrations, times of stress and pain, as well as moments of rejoicing, to accomplish that. May we all be people who long to look to him and know him better in all the mundane moments and frustrations, as well as the easier days.

§

7. New wineskins

I'm going to share one last story in this chapter about the way God changes us over time. Perhaps this particular aspect is the hardest area of our lives to submit to Jesus and to learn from his ways. What does it mean to forgive others, especially when we have been terribly wronged? I interviewed **Destiny** over the phone, and I could hear it profoundly in her voice. She has spent decades on this hardest lesson of all. She has not found it easy or simple. It's a daily, dependent lesson – to be able to forgive and to be a person who lets God's love pour out from our souls.

> 'It's been a really long journey, but I know that God is faithful. In 2002, my daughter died. It was a hot December day. She was 29. I can't describe it to you. My son saw it first on the TV. There had been a murder in Goondiwindi. The police rang and said the words every parent dreads hearing. "I'm sorry to inform you that your daughter has been murdered." We found out later that five people were responsible. Three of them are still in jail, including her ex-husband – my son-in-law. There's so much I could tell you – so much pain. It's a big, long, awful story. She left three children, aged eight, nine and 11. At first the children lived with me, and then they lived with my other daughter.
>
> The court case was a year or two later. We found out that drugs and alcohol were the fuel for it. Somehow, after the court case, I walked over to my son-in-law and I eyeballed him. I asked him how he was. Later, I took the kids to see him in jail. None of us knew what to say. But I kept going back to see him, regularly … and eventually he said sorry. He was repentant. He was on

> suicide watch. He asked me if I could forgive him. I can't say when it happened, but from the first day, I knew I wanted to forgive him. Over time, I did. I believe it was a gift from God. I could never do it myself. God did something in my heart, and it's been a release. It's been healing. If I hadn't been able to forgive, I know I would've been consumed by hatred and bitterness. It's been a long journey over 20 years, and some of our family members are still wrestling with it. I tell them that forgiveness isn't easy. It doesn't mean you ever have to see the person again. You don't have to come up with the strength yourself. You can say to God, "I can't do this."
>
> Sometimes I say to people I wish I had the answers. I don't. I don't know why God allows things. All I know is that he loves us, and that when hard things happen, God hurts as well. In those times, he wants us to press harder into him. Lately, we've been singing a song at church all about tears and sorrows and trusting in Jesus. That's my testimony. I'm 74 and I've had many tears and sorrows, but I've learnt to trust in God.'

As Destiny so honestly expresses, there are many things we will never understand. There is tragedy, unbearable pain, grief and human culpability. We don't have the right words or answers. But we can come to the cross. We can tell God we can't do it. We can kneel there and weep. We can see the Lord Jesus, who was the perfect Lamb of God, a righteous man without sin, and yet condemned for us to bring us to God. Jesus was flogged, mocked and crucified for us. Amazingly, as he hung there on the cross, Jesus spoke words of forgiveness to the crowd. Even in that moment, he was reconciling the ones who were nailing him to

7. New wineskins

the cross. He said, 'Father, forgive them, for they do not know what they are doing' (Luke 23:34).

And his words included us. Jesus bore our sins and the sins of the world. He forgave us. He carried our pain and questions. Then he gave up his spirit for us. He breathed his last breath. Somehow, as we receive this incredible forgiveness from God, we are also given the merciful gift of being able to offer forgiveness to others, even those who have done terrible wrong to us. But as Destiny rightly says, it isn't easy. It isn't our work. It may take an entire lifetime. Today, though, we can thank God that he offers us complete, unimaginable forgiveness, and we can pray that he would help us to forgive.

Like Destiny, and so many others I interviewed, there was also a remarkable testimony to the truth that suffering can soften us, mature our empathy and expand our faith as we lean on Jesus. May we each be encouraged by these stories of God at work in human lives, changing us and conforming us slowly to God's image everywhere – at work, at home, in prison, in ministry and in crisis. May we also continue to be people who offer every part of our lives back to God for his redemptive purposes.

8
Go, pour out your gift

Gathering 300 faith stories reminded me of something else wonderfully important. The journey of following Jesus is not just about years of submitting to God's Spirit in an ever-growing, transformative way; it also becomes a journey of longing to pour out our gifts daily in response to God's great, consuming love for us.

It's a tremendous, ongoing privilege. As I said in chapter 1, I remember sitting in my bed, reading John 15:12 for the first time, aged 12: 'My command is this: love each other as I have loved you.' I sat there and wondered ... what does it mean to love others as God had loved me? How does a 12-year-old lay down her life for her friends?

The answers, in each individual life, become as varied as the stars in the sky. That's the wonderful thing. We've seen it in all the faith stories that we've read so far. Scott and Janelle went off to serve God in Cambodia. Kaz set up a comfy, red lounge in the back of her shop for people in need. Melissa began work with drug addicts. Bec and Memo became part of a ministry helping refugees in Sydney. Mike felt led to teach theology at a Melbourne Bible college. Allan began serving people in his retirement village in Lithgow, helping them with their tech issues. Every person, as a follower of Jesus, also longs to pour out their heart in love because they know they've been loved beyond compare. They know that all the gifts they've been given have come from God.

Our service in God's kingdom takes many different forms and styles over the decades of life. It keeps changing! After our six years in Nepal, Darren, our three sons and I returned to Australia and enjoyed 16 years living in the Blue Mountains, west of Sydney. It was a stable and fruitful time. During those years, Darren lectured at Sydney University, and we loved our local church. We regularly visited Nepal as well as other countries, story-gathering, writing, speaking and being surprised by God.

About a year ago, Darren and I moved again, this time from the Blue Mountains to a smaller town in the Central West of New South Wales, which we love. I'll describe that a bit more in chapter 10. But a bigger change for us has been becoming 'empty nesters.' All of our three sons have now moved out of home, which has freed up our time. We're asking God about the next season. What should we do now? How can we best use the gifts that we've been given now and the experiences God has allowed us to live through in Nepal and Australia? Are there new opportunities to serve him strategically, as well as day-to-day opportunities in our activities and relationships?

Sometimes, I find that the more opportunities there are around me, the more confused I become. I know that Darren and I need to stop and seek God's leading more this year in prayer. I also know that sometimes God makes the path very clear, and at other times, less so. Sometimes, God asks us to make good and godly decisions based on what we know of him and how he's led us so far. Often, God uses the challenges that we've lived through to uniquely serve others, as was the case with Kaz, Melissa, Cameron, Destiny and many others.

I find it so encouraging to read these examples, reminding me that God enables each of us to draw from the deep wells of our experience and point to Jesus.

I'd love to share a few more examples of the ways that people have responded to the love of God by pouring out their gifts, often in sacrificial ways. In each of the following stories, the person has been open to Jesus and obedient to his command to take up their cross and deny themselves. Sometimes, as I said, the opportunity to serve has arisen from their own experiences. At other times, the opportunity to minister has come right out of the blue. That was the case for our friends **Mick** and **Kara**. We'll hear from Mick first.

> 'About 15 years ago, a friend invited me to join a Bible study group. I said, "No, thanks, that sounds pretty boring. If I was going to read the Bible, I'd read the Bible by myself."
>
> Back then, I wasn't regularly going to church or reading the Bible. My wife, Kara, was going to church, but I used to stay at home. I was living my own life, working long hours as a project manager and making a home-brew in our spare room.
>
> But then I thought ... if I told my friend that I can read the Bible by myself, maybe I should? So, the next week, I went off in my lunch hour, and I bought myself a Bible and a Bible-reading plan. I started reading, beginning with the Gospel of Luke. The words leapt off the page and gripped my heart. Luke 1 is not a particularly evangelistic passage, but I felt convicted by the truth of God's word and overwhelmed by God's presence.
>
> I went home and I told Kara. She was amazed! God changed me from that moment on. I stopped swearing without even

> thinking about it. I eventually even cleaned up the room I'd been using to make the home-brew. Kara wondered what was going on. I started going to church, and I asked people how I could serve there. I started to pray. It just flowed out. It was the power of God's word at work in my life. I kept doing the same long hours at work (usually 12 hours a day), but I signed up to do a Bible college course by correspondence. I would sit there every night, studying the Bible.
>
> And one night, while I was reading my Bible (and the fire was going and the dog was on the floor), I saw a vision of a Muslim man. I heard a voice repeatedly telling me to go. He kept saying, "Go, go, go."
>
> I did a double-take. I checked that I was awake. I was definitely awake. The next morning, I told Kara. She wasn't as convinced as I was, and it took us many years to prepare … but the thought of people not having access to the Bible and the gospel of Jesus, and its power to change lives, drove me every day. We ended up leaving Australia and serving in the Muslim world for six years. Now we're back in Australia with the same calling. We're serving with an organisation here, reaching out to those who haven't heard about Jesus yet …'

I love Mick's story. As soon as he read Luke 1, he was convinced of God's truth, and it changed him so much that he immediately wanted to go and serve. How could he not? It just flowed out of him. And then he saw the vision of the Muslim man, and he heard the compelling message to go and serve in the Muslim world, where there was so little access to the Bible.

Kara's response was quite different, and we'll hear about that next. But it's also good to pause and remember the words from Paul in Romans 10:13: 'Everyone who calls on the name of the Lord will be saved.' But how can they call if they haven't heard? And how can they hear unless someone speaks? And how can someone speak unless they are sent?

Of course, we are now living in an age when digital technology and the movement of people groups have changed the challenges and the opportunities. We have cross-cultural opportunities everywhere without needing a passport, visa or aeroplane ticket. Yet, there is still a great need for people to go and share the wonderful news, the gospel of grace, in every part of the world and indeed at the ends of our streets.

I love the way that Mick himself heard the transformative message of God's grace and then was gripped by the need to tell others. I also love how surprised **Kara** was! Let's hear her side of the story.

> 'One day, my husband, Mick, came home and said to me, "I think we're being called to serve in the Muslim world." It was completely out of the blue for me. I hadn't had the same revelation. I needed to think and pray. We had three small children, and we were living "the dream" in our local community in the Blue Mountains, west of Sydney – renovating our house and being involved in our local church. I said that I needed time to think about it. Mick was only recently committed as a Christian! He'd had a major turnaround in his life through reading the Bible, and he suddenly became passionately committed to serving in a place where the Bible wasn't easily accessible. But it took longer for me. Overseas mission wasn't

even on my radar. I was comfortable! I couldn't imagine living in a Muslim country.

So, I talked with a Christian friend, and she said, "You won't hear from God unless you're soaked in the word." So, I did that. I immersed myself in the Bible for the next 18 months. I read through the Gospels and Hebrews. I prayed and prayed. One of the things that stood out to me was the story of Sarah. She went with Abraham, even though she didn't know where they were going, and they lived in a tent. And the same with Peter – he stepped off the boat in Matthew 14, even though he must have been worried. But he tried to keep his eyes on Jesus. And in some ways, I felt like the life I was living in our renovated home was my "safe boat". How could I leave it? But I wanted to have the same sort of faith as Sarah or Peter. I wanted to fix my eyes on Jesus.

Then one day, I read Acts 20:24, "However, I consider my life worth nothing to me; my only aim is to finish the race and complete the task the Lord Jesus has given me – the task of testifying to the good news of God's grace."

That's when I changed. I realised that the "good life" we were living in the Blue Mountains was only good because Jesus had made it good. He had turned our lives around and given us everything we had … so we needed to choose the way we could use that good life for him. We wanted to testify to his grace, wherever he led us. I had to be willing to go. I had to value him (and his grace) more than my safe, comfortable place.

> Five years later, we went and lived among the people in a particular country in the Muslim world. It was amazing!'

I love the advice that Kara's friend gave her. Soak yourself in God's word. Read the Bible deeply. As you do, you will remember God's heart and his mission. As you dwell on his word, your decisions will become clearer. It's so true. Kara wasn't immediately keen. She had many questions. But as she soaked herself in God's word over 18 months, the answers became clear to her. Everything she had was a gift from God, so that she could pour it out.

I personally relate to Kara's story. On many occasions, since arriving back in Australia from Nepal, I have struggled with the same questions. What should we do now? Will we move countries again? Will I focus on this piece of writing or something new? Will I agree to that new invitation or opportunity? I desperately want clear leading from God and get frustrated when it doesn't appear to be that simple. And then, every time, the answers are the same: slow down. Pray. Soak yourself in God's word. Remember his heart for his world. Remember his priorities for his people. Remember that everything you have is a gift from God ... and that he invites, enables and strengthens us to love him and others in the ways he has in mind. Ultimately, keeping our eyes on him and following his leading is so much better than staying in our own safe boat! Let's pray that we can each soak ourselves in God's word today, letting it speak to our souls.

§

I remember when I was at Bible college, back in the early 90s, there was a sense that the needs of the world for the gospel were mostly in developing countries, or what was referred to at the time as the third world. But even back then, there was a hint that it might be changing. Perhaps there would come a day when Asia and Africa would be sending missionaries back to the West. Imagine that? Of course, we now live in an era when that is happening in wonderful ways, praise God. We have so much to learn from our brothers and sisters all around the world. Here is **Emmah**'s story.

> 'I grew up in a village in Kenya. When I was seven years old, I had an encounter with God. I was in a room by myself, singing a song I'd learnt at Sunday school. Suddenly the room was filled with the awesome presence of God. I started crying. It was so peaceful. I said, "God, I know you're real, and you're here. I know you love me. Please forgive me."
>
> It was a life-changing moment. Afterwards, I told my mum and she just looked at me – she didn't seem to understand my experience. From that day on, though, I knew that God existed. I had a passionate desire to serve him. After school, I went to university in Nairobi, and I studied commerce. I still recall God providing for me miraculously. It was an expensive university, and I wondered how to pay the school fees. One day, the financial aid officer called me, out of the blue, and said that the university should give me a scholarship. I didn't even know the university gave scholarships!
>
> During those years at university, God started speaking to me about Australia. I don't know why he did. All I knew about Australia was in *Home and Away* and *Neighbours*. But God's voice was so clear to me. He said, "I have work for you to do in Australia."

I put it aside for a long time. I met my husband and married him. We had three kids. I got a good job working for the Kenyan government and then for the United Nations. My husband worked as an architect. We were settled in our own home. We were very happy. I really, really love Africa! At the same time, one of my colleagues was from Melbourne. He said, "Stay in Kenya! People are so happy and friendly here!"

I agreed with him, but God kept putting Australia on my heart. Then God said it was time. Everything came together. Our pastor in Kenya went to Australia, and he came back and asked my husband and me whether we would consider going to Australia to do mission work.

I resigned from my job, and we started preparing. We went to Bible college. God was working in our hearts. It's funny, because normally people come from Australia and Europe to Africa for mission. We were being led the other way around. God kept saying to us that he wanted us to partner with him in what he was already doing in Australia.

We arrived here in 2017, with nine suitcases. We had no jobs, but we had visas, and we found a rental place and my husband found a job in architecture. Our kids settled in school. It felt like God was working in miraculous ways. We experienced a lot of kindness in Australia. The people here are very kind to foreigners.

After some months, God started giving me opportunities to work here with the churches through 'Greater West for Christ'. There is so much spiritual need in Australia. When missionaries

> go to Africa, they often provide food and medical assistance because there is physical need. In Australia, there is great spiritual need. People have everything they need, but they don't have rest or quietness. There is restlessness and anxiety and depression. People are seeking happiness in having things or doing things. They're putting their confidence in their own abilities. But we have to realise we can't do everything, and we must depend on Jesus. We can't solve all our problems, and we must put our confidence in Jesus!
>
> In Exodus, Pharaoh said to Moses, "Who is the Lord, that I should obey him?" (5:2). Pharaoh had also created a system that was very efficient. He thought he didn't need God. But it can never work. It's an idol of self. We must find our rest and peace and confidence in Jesus. That's what I feel called to share. There are so many opportunities to serve God's people in Australia! I love this nation.'

Isn't that wonderful? From the first moment Emmah came to know Jesus, she felt a passionate desire to serve him. This desire continued to grow and evolve until God specifically led her to come to Australia. Over time, that leading was confirmed, and the family arrived here, excited to partner with what God was already doing. Slowly, God began giving Emmah ministry opportunities and insights into the mindset of Australians – that we are in great need of spiritual rest and quietness. We often have everything we need materially, but we don't have peace with God. We rely on ourselves.

Since hearing Emmah's faith story, I've often reflected on her insights and agreed with them! Sometimes it takes an outsider to notice a general state of mind in a society, especially when the observer comes from a different cultural background and has a fresh perspective on God's truth. We need to hear these insights! Emmah's service has been such a blessing to the people in her new church and community in Western Sydney.

I also appreciate Emmah's thoughts on confidence. The writer of Hebrews mentions confidence quite a lot. It's such an important thing to have. But it's easy, especially in the West, to put our confidence in everything else – our own abilities and resources. And it can never work. As Emmah says, it's an idol of self. Instead, have confidence in Christ! (Heb 10:35–37). Jesus is our great high priest, and he has entered the most holy place, offering himself as a sacrifice. Because of that, we can draw near to God and speak to him today. We can approach God with confidence. *Lord, we come to you and ask for that deep confidence in Christ. Please let it slow us down today. Let it bring rest and quietness. Let it speak to our scattered hearts, reminding us to depend on you alone.*

§

Of course, not every time we participate in God's mission for the world will involve overseas relocation. Most often, we will have our eyes opened to the needs around us, in the places where God has allowed us to be. As we do that, God will show us the ways we can use our gifts, in beautiful, fresh ways, as **Sam** discovered.

> 'In my 20s, my husband and I moved to Deniliquin (country New South Wales) to be near his parents. We had two young children. I was reading a lot of New Age material, and I had a lot of life questions. Such as what are we here for? Sometime

later, I was talking to my mother-in-law about all my questions, and she said, very graciously, "Did you know … that everything you're seeking, you can find in Jesus?"

The next morning was a challenging morning. My young daughter was incredibly upset, and we were all very stressed. My mother-in-law left for work, but on her way out, she said, "There's a book on the kitchen bench and there's a prayer on the back page. You might read it and see if you feel like saying it."

I picked it up and I read the prayer. I prayed it. The peace I felt was phenomenal. It overcame the whole house. Even my daughter and her demeanour were changed. It was beautiful!

After that, I started going to a playgroup with my children at the local church. One of the ladies met with me to disciple me one-on-one. It was amazing. I joined a Bible study, and I went to church.

But it was a few years later that things really started going 100 miles an hour. My mother-in-law, a close friend and I had all been challenged by the call to minister in our own neighbourhood. We recognised we had been a bit insular. We decided to start a community kitchen. It was partly because of our giftings. The three of us all loved to cook!

We started on Wednesday nights, serving a meal to the local community at 5:30 pm. The first night, one woman came. We were so excited! We served her dinner and dessert. Then the next Wednesday a few more people came, and then it grew from word of mouth. It just took off. We've been doing it now

> for 12 years, every Wednesday night, and we get anything from 30 people up to 100. Most of our "kitchen family" haven't got a church background. Many of them have mental health issues. A lot of them are lonely, or elderly, or in the lower income category. We just welcome them. We love them and we chat with them, and we serve them. I pray before the meal and ask them if they have prayer requests. We've had some amazing conversations – with people who wouldn't normally talk about Jesus or ask for prayer.
>
> Two years ago, we started doing Bible study after the meal. Guess who was the first to come. The same woman who came on the first night. That made me teary. Now, we get a whole range of people. At first, I didn't have a lot of confidence. I've had to step out of my comfort zone. But God is extremely gracious. He has shown me that it's in my weakness that he works. He says, "My grace is sufficient for you, for my power is made perfect in weakness" (2 Cor 12:9). These days, I also help to lead a church on Sundays that is associated with the kitchen. I am beyond excited to see what God has done through me, but even more so, to see what he's doing through those he's brought alongside me to fellowship at our church.'

It's a brilliant story. When I spoke with Sam and heard her story of faith, she was bubbling over with what God had done in her life. It all began with reading the prayer in the book, thanks to her mother-in-law, and then feeling a phenomenal peace. Sam came to know Jesus and grew in her faith. But she was especially excited about the community meals. After sensing God's leading and the clear challenge to serve their local community, she and her helpers have been providing these three-course meals as gifts to anyone who comes, simply as an expression of love. They've been doing it weekly for 12 years! And a lot of people have been coming. Out of the meals, a Bible study has grown, and then a church gathering made up of many people who wouldn't normally ever go to church. I love the way God works! He prompts us to serve him using the gifts he has already given us. He works in people's hearts. He brings joy. And he enables. His grace is sufficient for each of us, even when we find ourselves doing something that is way out of our comfort zones.

As well as leading the church gathering that has grown out of the Wednesday night meals, Sam also works full-time and cares for her own family. I asked her how she finds the time, and she said, 'I have to rely on God!' That's the best answer, isn't it? May we each find that God's grace is sufficient for our needs today, especially when we're feeling inadequate or pushed out of our insular corners. Even more than that, may the people who normally feel most excluded from our church gatherings find a lovely, surprising welcome today.

§

It's true that God gifts his people to serve him in the world. And we go, feeling compelled and enabled to share his gospel message with the people in our streets who so desperately need to hear it. But because we're human, we also feel small and frail and scared. We are usually very aware of our own weaknesses and inadequacies. We often worry about what other people may think of us. That's the reality of service – the strange combination of pathetic humans serving a glorious God who is able. But it's at the intersection of that combination that beautiful things can happen. **Ray**'s story is the perfect example of that.

'I was a Chief Petty Officer on the *HMAS Perth* in 1982. We were patrolling in the Indian Ocean, during the Iran–Iraq War. But a few years before that, I'd become a Christian at a Billy Graham Crusade. So, I knew it was going to be really hard being back at sea as a Christian. There were 300 people on the ship, and they could shred me.

Just before I went, I was memorising verses … and one of them was 1 Corinthians 10:13: "No temptation has overtaken you except what is common to mankind. And God is faithful; he will not let you be tempted beyond what you can bear." I prayed to God. And then I took a whole bunch of Christian books with me on the ship.

When we were out at sea, I asked the captain if I could hold a regular Bible study. He said yes. So, every week, I would make an announcement about the Bible study on the ship's PA system, from the bridge to the whole ship, at 6:45 pm. It had never been done before. But that wasn't the hard part. The hard part was picking up my Bible and walking through the ship, past everyone eating, and everyone looking up and staring at me, the Christian. Every night, I said I can't do it. Then I prayed to God and asked him to help me and give me courage.

The first week, I went up to the room and waited. One other guy came. It was just him and me for the first few weeks, reading the Bible. Then someone else came to have a look. By the end of six months, there were 12 to 15 guys coming every week – officers and sailors. It was standing room only. They all wanted to know more about Jesus. They were reading the

> Bible and praying together. One guy gave his life to the Lord. It was so exciting. I had thought I was going to be crushed and isolated, and yet I found they respected me. And I found the truth in that verse. God helped me and he gave me courage ... and he brought people into his kingdom.'

Praise God for the way he worked on that ship and through Ray's witness! But it's true that as humans, we worry. We worry that if we tell anyone we have faith in Jesus, they might ridicule us or think less of us. And sometimes, they might! We might indeed lose jobs, relationships or respect. But even so, like Ray, there will be times when we might choose to talk publicly about Jesus. We might invite our colleagues to Bible study. We might feel scared or worried that we'll say the wrong things and put people off. But within all of that strange human dynamic and our own insecurities, God works for good, in his timing, sometimes in ways beyond what we imagined.

I love Ray's story. He thought the other guys would ridicule him, and instead, they respected him. He thought he would be mocked, and instead, he was given courage. His colleagues were interested. They came to hear more about the Bible until it was standing room only. And God worked in their hearts, in the way that God does. May we each be compelled to pray that same prayer, especially on the days when we fear ridicule or shame – that we would be given courage in our places of work and witness, and that God would work in people's hearts through his wonderful, upside-down gospel message, all for his glory.

§

It's a wonderful truth that God uses whatever gifts he has given us, in the places he puts us, to point to him, if we make ourselves available to him. Here's a story from our friend **Mark**, who not only looks like Elvis Presley but sings like him too.

> 'I grew up in Malta up to the age of nine years old, listening to Elvis on the radio. Elvis Presley is treated like a God in Malta. Then, as an adult, I became a Christian in New Zealand, and I started doing Elvis tributes and concerts – professionally and for ministry. I called it Born Again Elvis. When I moved to Australia, I met my wife and we did Elvis concerts together – three or four events every weekend – cruises, weddings, birthday parties and christenings. It went on for 20 years. We used it for an income and also for ministry, to share the gospel. During the show, I'd always tell my life story – how I became a Christian – and I'd sing snippets of Elvis songs that related to that part of the story. We would always sing 'Amazing Grace' at the end of the show, and then I'd minister to people afterwards. People always want to talk with Elvis! They think that he's the king. But we tell them about Jesus, the real King! I loved it. I also went to Bible college and trained as a pastor.
>
> Then, in 2017, we left for Malta, long-term, for mission with European Christian Mission (ECM). I thought we'd do music ministry and Elvis concerts there. But now we've been in Malta for three years, and we haven't actually used Elvis a huge amount. In some ways, it's been hard. Elvis was a huge part of my identity. But it's funny, because at one of the few Elvis

concerts we did, we saw a Maltese lady actually come to the Lord. It was an 80th birthday party, and the lady was the grand-niece of the 80-year-old. Through a relationship with our family, she has come to faith in Jesus. We recently baptised her, and we are discipling her. It was God's grace to us ... one of the few times we did an Elvis event!

But when it was hard and I was missing doing the concerts, I read Romans 8: "And we know that in all things God works for the good of those who love him, who have been called according to his purpose" (v. 28). I had to surrender it to Jesus. And Jesus is so kind to us. At the moment, we're back in Sydney, quarantining in the Meriton Hotel because of COVID. It was a big thing to get back here after being bumped off our flight in Heathrow. We thought we might not get another flight to Australia till next March! But here we are, and it's amazing. It turns out that my cousin manages the food at this hotel, and his boss is a Christian. So, he told her that I'm a pastor and I do Elvis concerts, and so she started witnessing to him about Jesus, and she keeps sending us Scripture notes in the food. It's fantastic! The challenge for me, though, is to keep trusting Jesus for his purposes. We plan things, but he's the one who brings about his purposes. God is so sovereign! And he wants us to be like him, to be a blessing, to be like Jesus to other people, like the lady sending Scripture notes. We can be like that too, on mission wherever we are!'

This is beautiful, isn't it? We can be on mission for Jesus wherever we are – whether serving with ECM in Malta, singing at sold-out Elvis concerts in Sydney or quarantined in the Meriton Hotel during a pandemic, wondering what on earth God is doing. What I love about Mark's story is his beautiful uniqueness. I don't know anyone else in the world who is engaged in gospel ministry through doing Elvis Presley tribute concerts. But for anyone who knows Mark, you will know how perfectly this ministry suits him!

At the same time, it strikes me that Mark is saying the same thing as so many of the others who have shared their faith stories. We don't know what's ahead, but we can trust God. We must depend on him. We may not understand what he has in mind or even want it, but we are assured that God knows! And as we trust him, surprising and wonderful things may happen. Unexpected opportunities might arise, even while in strict quarantine in a hotel room in Sydney during a pandemic. I love the way God works, often bringing strangers together who then overflow with the goodness of Jesus to the people around them.

That's the thing: it's the love of Jesus that compels us to speak, act, love and serve, pointing to him, whether we're in Sydney or Malta. We know for sure that Jesus died for us so that we might live. We know for sure that he was raised from the dead. And so, we share of his love, whether we're singing Elvis songs on a grand stage, walking down a quiet street with one person or hanging out in a hotel room in quarantine. Like Mark, we can be a blessing to other people wherever we are.

§

I'd love to share another example of the way God uses even the hard things in our lives to bless others in need. In God's economy, every single season we live through is a preparation for the one to come.

8. Go, pour out your gift

This has certainly been the case for **Les**, who told me about his childhood spent with his father in and out of prison.

> 'Sadly, the home I grew up in was domestically violent. My father was a petty thief and a compulsive liar. He had a few spells in prison. When I was five, the police came and arrested him for stolen goods that he'd given to us as Christmas presents. He would steal clothes from our neighbour's clotheslines and give them to us … and then tell us not to make friends. We might be wearing their clothes.
>
> I left school at 14 and got a job at Woolies to help Mum feed us. During my time there, I had a wonderful boss. I couldn't add up, but he moved me to the mail room. He became like a surrogate dad. He encouraged me to do night school – a leaving certificate and then later a business management degree.
>
> During that time, I noticed a young man walking past our house on his way to church. His name was Arthur. He invited us to youth group, and I started going. I hadn't heard of Jesus before, except as a swear word. We had a Bible in our house, but it was used as a weapon. I went to youth group, and suddenly I had friends! It was a lot of fun, and I got more involved. Then Arthur invited us to beach mission. I was exposed to a Christian community for the first time, and I read John 3:16. I came to faith in Jesus!
>
> A few years later, I left Woolies and started working with kids at risk. That's been my heart my whole life. My first job was at a youth centre in Green Valley. Within four days, I was assaulted … and in hospital getting my face rearranged. There were a lot

of tough kids, and it was an initiation process. But I loved it! I loved the kids. They had nothing – no home, no recreation, no God. We developed a camps program, coffee shops, safe-driver training and sports programs …

After 40 years of working with kids at risk, as well as my normal work, I retired. The next day, I walked into the Scripture Union office, and I said, "I'm here. How can I help?" They said, "How would you like to run camps for kids whose parents are in prison?" Scripture Union had been invited by Prison Fellowship to conduct these camps.

When I was a kid, I had visited my father in prison. I remember standing behind a yellow line and speaking to him through a wire fence. I had also run many camps as part of my youth work. We started the program. They were tough kids! Sometimes, it was challenging to find them. The parents were incarcerated, but the government doesn't keep a record of the kids. They're forgotten. They're tough, but they're crying out for affection. The work is slow.

After the first six camps, our organisation became Second Chances, South Australia, and we became the sole provider of the camps.

Thirteen years ago, I invited a young Indigenous Australian boy to camp. He was 11 years old, living with his nanna, who adopted him. You could tell he was a survivor. He knew how to fight back. It was a hard week, but I sat next to him. I told him I knew what it was like. He told me his nanna was sick. A week later, she died.

> Thirteen years later, that boy is 24. He's now working with youth and community services. He said he wanted to be like me. If I've done nothing else in my life, I've been his friend. He invited me to his 21st a few years ago. I invited him to my 80th last month. A year ago, he said he wanted "to give God a go", and now he wants to go to Bible college. There have been others like him, of course, but he's my highlight!
>
> Nowadays, I have Psalm 86:11 written over my kitchen sink: "Teach me your way, LORD, that I may rely on your faithfulness." I tell the kids, "When I was your age, I didn't have God to help me, because I didn't know him. But you can know him, and he can help you now!"'

There is so much to enjoy in Les' story, isn't there? God not only prepared Les to work with kids at risk but also gave him great joy and delight in doing so. He loved it! And God continued to give Les opportunities throughout his life, even into retirement, as he directed Les to spend time with children whose parents were in prison, just as Les' own father had been in prison. But the loveliest part to me is the delight that Les described in having that one particular friend. No doubt, he has impacted hundreds of young people through his decades of ministry, but he thinks if he's done nothing else, he's been a friend to one young Indigenous Australian boy who now wants to go to Bible college. That's wonderful!

May we each be encouraged by the way God works in our lives, and may we bring him delight in our service. May we each find great joy in serving Jesus with the unique sets of gifts and experiences that he's given us, as well as the challenges he has allowed us to live through.

As a side note, I find it particularly encouraging to hear the willingness and generosity in Les' heart. The day after he stopped paid work, after 40 years, he walked straight into the Scripture Union office and said, 'What can I do to help?' May God also grow willing and generous hearts in each of us, this year and beyond.

§

Of course, our desire to be involved in organised ministry is not always straightforward. It does not always work out the way we want. **Kirk**'s story is a needed example of that.

> 'I have a tendency to be ambitious and driven … or idealistic, perhaps, so I need to watch that these tendencies don't slip into my motivations for ministry. Years ago, I had to pause before starting training for ministry because I needed to sort out the importance of serving God out of freedom and joy, not to somehow make myself more acceptable to God.
>
> Given this background, it has been no small thing to experience plans changing and even being blocked. Our family story has involved years of caring for one son with uncontrolled epilepsy, experiencing the death of a daughter with anencephaly and managing my own episodes of clinical depression and anxiety. The son with epilepsy is now a young man, and he needs care with most activities due to intellectual impairment and autism.
>
> Proverbs 19:21 says "Many are the plans in a person's heart, but it is the Lord's purpose that prevails." It seems that I need to keep learning that.

Along the way, I have had the chance to engage with sections of the Old Testament in depth because of my work in preaching at church and in lecturing at SMBC [Sydney Missionary and Bible College]. The book of Deuteronomy is precious in showing me the lavish graciousness of God's love and his commitment to doing good for his people, including the way he sets up a society that creates a just and open-handed community. The book of Isaiah is important to me. Not only do I find its clever crafting of poetry and storytelling very moving, but I keep getting amazed at how God's intentions to save cannot be stopped. The ways that God saves are surprising in the book. It may be through a little child, or a king who looks sick or weak, or even through a foreigner who temporarily carries the title 'Messiah'. God's ways are not what we always expect. I have also had occasion to sit closely with the book of Job for years. Its vision of creation especially fascinates me. Under the good hand of the Lord, creation is wild, dangerous and inefficient, but endlessly fascinating and beautiful. In a similar way, Ecclesiastes has taught me that there is an intrinsic fragility and transience to life. While this can make us frustrated and sad, it also means that little pleasures and moments of beauty can be received for what they are: fleeting gifts, beyond our control but full of joy and grace.

Over the years, I've come to see that whether we think about creation or God's story of redemption, God moves toward his world with deep grace. I see this in the Bible, and as I look up, I see it in the world, in his people and in the life that God has brought to me through Jesus.

> At the moment, my wife and I are embarking on a new plan. We would love to start a Christian community for people with disabilities, with an aim to encourage a world where people are drawn to the outsider and the marginalised, where disability is not seen as a mistake, where there is an understanding of God being present in what we might describe as the worst of experiences, and where people grow in their trust of Jesus … through whom God knows the experience of disability more than we might think. Of course, yet again, I must learn to hold this plan lightly, knowing that it is the Lord's purpose that prevails.'

Kirk's story is real and vulnerable. He admits that he has struggled with his own heart motivation for ministry as well as numerous layers of disrupted plans. The disruptions have been hard and ongoing, even in the three years since sharing his faith story. Yet, as we read Kirk's story, we nod along with him. We, too, have experienced disruption of plans. We, too, need to absorb those same profound truths about the nature of God, who is present with us in the hardest of times and knows the experience of frailty and disability more than we might imagine.

Like Kirk, I have always found the book of Ecclesiastes very refreshing. Its pages are so full of honest human questions, and most of them are confronting. Why are we here? What's the point of all this endless toil and rain? Who gains anything from this ceaseless rhythm? And yet also, within the confronting nature of the writing and questions, there is a time to pause and agree. Yes, we do see fragility, transience and unpredictability all around us. Yes, our lives are fleeting and we're not in control. At the deepest level, we know who is in control: 'I know that everything God does will endure for ever; nothing can be added to it and nothing taken from it. God does it so that people will fear him' (Eccl 3:14). Like Kirk, we can find rest in God's character, and we can notice simple beauty. We can enjoy the feel of sunshine on our skin, the taste of pizza for lunch or the sight of a pink dahlia moving in the breeze ... as we humbly plan our next project or ministry idea. Most of all, we can know, deeply, that God moves towards us with deep grace every day, even when we're not even aware of it.

§

I'd like to share one more story of plans unexpectedly changing and the impact it can have on ministry. **Gill** spent 17 years in Tanzania, and she was planning on staying there for life. She didn't know that God had something else in mind.

> 'My big conversion was in Tanzania. Before that, I was a nominal Christian. I knew all the facts. I'd gone to a Billy Graham Crusade in 1961. I went to Tanzania in 1974 as a missionary with CMS [Church Missionary Society], and that's where I understood grace for the first time. I worked as a secretary for two different bishops. But just before I left for Tanzania, someone had given me a copy of *Knowing God* by Jim Packer. I still remember the day. I was in my bedroom, and I got the book out to read, and I suddenly realised that the God of the universe had chosen me before the foundation of the world ... and I had to do nothing. Before that, I'd seen Christianity as a list of things I had to do, and I didn't always measure up. I'd tried to be the good daughter/good missionary, and it didn't always work. But that day, I got grace. I suddenly saw that it

wasn't about me being good or anything at all. Jesus had done it for me. It was as if I'd never heard the gospel before. I got down on my knees and I prayed. And afterwards, I kept going back to that chapter ... as well as the Bible!

The rest of my years in Tanzania were really positive. After three years, my language was good. I could listen to Swahili and "hear" what it meant. All my close friends were Africans. I was involved in a girls' club, and in one place I ran the local church bookshop. In other places, I just helped out wherever I could. I was planning on staying in Tanzania for life.

Then, after 17 years in Tanzania, my twin sister called me from Australia. It was January 1991, and she was struggling. She said, "I have this sense that I need you at home, nearby." Her husband had died 10 years earlier and she had three teenage children. She'd also had Hodgkin Disease many years earlier, and her health was deteriorating.

I talked with my boss and my bishop. They agreed that I should return to Australia, so I left in April after a most amazing farewell. When I arrived, I went straight to my sister's place to look after her kids while she went to Sydney for an assessment. It turned out that her heart tissue was fibrosed from the radiotherapy, and she couldn't get on the list for a heart transplant. She died three months later, in July of that year. She was 45.

I inherited her kids and they inherited me, but it actually felt like we chose each other. It was a hard start, though. I was known to them, but I knew nothing about teenagers ... and we were all grieving. I was juggling everything and working out boundaries. It was very hard. I'd never even changed a nappy.

> For a long time, I just put one foot in front of the other. I'd wake up, get out of bed and then do it all again the next day. The thing that helped me most was going to church. People there were very helpful. And that's where I cried. We would be singing a song or a hymn, and I would just cry. There was one hymn in particular. "How good is the God we adore, our faithful, unchangeable friend! … We'll praise him for all that is past and trust him for all that's to come."
>
> That hymn sustained me every single day. It reverberated in my heart and mind. I've asked my friends to play it at my funeral. And good things happened as well. I got a job, which was a miracle. Then many years later, I became involved in a church that had people from many cultures. One day, a new family came from Africa. I went over and greeted the lady in her mother tongue. It turned out she'd lived in a refugee camp in Tanzania before arriving in Australia. She was amazed! She thought she'd never hear her mother tongue spoken ever again!
>
> And now it's been 30 years since I returned to Australia. The kids are all in their 40s and we're all such good friends … it's amazing!'

It's a needed reminder. Every single time, the most important thing is our heart response to God and our desire to serve him, rather than the geographical location we find ourselves in. God enabled Gill to serve him in Tanzania for 17 years. He equally enabled her to come home to Australia, just at the right time, and love those three orphaned teenagers. There is a wonderful truth in Philippians 2:13: '… it is God who works in you to will and to act in order to fulfil his good purpose.' It is also true that God can redeem the hardest parts of our lives and turn them into a new kind of service. I can imagine how hard it was for Gill to be thrown into parenting three teenagers after more than 40 years of singleness. No wonder she sang that hymn repeatedly and cried at church. I would have done the same.

But the postscript is very important. God was with her. He gave her paid work, miraculously, and enabled her to serve and love the kids through all those hard years. He also led Gill to a church in Sydney where people from many different cultures congregated, including one lovely family straight from a refugee camp in Tanzania. I'd love to have been a fly on the wall that day when they arrived in Australia, went to church and immediately met Gill, who spoke to them in their mother tongue. I also wonder how Gill's nieces and nephews now describe their story, 40 years after the loss of their mother.

Thinking about the family from Tanzania and Gill's wider family reminds me that all our stories are connected in some way to thousands of other people and their stories. We don't live neat, isolated lives, and nor would we want to. God works his purposes through hard, unexpected times in communities and families. As he does so, we continue to trust him and sing about our faithful, unchangeable friend, as long as he gives us breath.

§

I'd love to share one last story about pouring out our gifts in response to God's great love for us. I met **Coral** a year ago, on a sunny day at her home on an acreage south of Bathurst. She was 89, and she had been teaching Scripture at her local school for 45 years. She said to me that she would love to keep teaching Scripture for as long as she can. As I write this, she still is!

8. Go, pour out your gift

'I was born and raised in Broken Hill. I went to church there, and all that, but it became real for me in 1949, when I was 15. Back then, Broken Hill used to have a Christian mission once a year – an open-air meeting on the street near the shops. An evangelist came from Sydney and gave a gospel message. He preached the cross of Jesus. I was really moved by it. I just realised Jesus did it for me; he died for me.

I was quite shy before that. But after I prayed the prayer of commitment to Jesus, I slowly came out of my shell. After school, I decided to go to a teacher's college in Bathurst, and after that, I thought I would be a missionary in Africa.

In my first years of teaching in Bathurst, I met my future husband at the social club at church. Ross was a farmer. I told him I was planning to be a missionary in Africa, and he said, "I feel God has given me this farm."

The farm was 730 acres, south of Bathurst. It had 500 sheep that were producing fine wool, and it grew vegetables that were sold at the markets.

Over the next three months, I prayed to God about it. During that time, I saw a gospel film about a boy whose parents wanted him to be a minister, but he felt God wanted him to fix cars, so he was a missionary at the local garage.

I wrote to Ross (there were no phones in those days) and I said, "I think I've got my answer." He came to see me in Broken Hill, and we got engaged. My parents loved him. My dad came into my bedroom early the next morning and said, "He's a man in a million – marry him."

We got engaged in 1957. Ross started making bricks straight away. He wanted to build me a new house on the farm. After we got married, we were both involved in the church. I didn't do any paid teaching, but we had four children, and I was very involved in the local school. Then, when our youngest was in high school, I offered to take on Scripture at two schools.

I've been teaching Scripture at Perthville Public School for 45 years now. I really enjoy it. I like telling stories, and I like the singing. It's rewarding when I meet some boy down the street, and he says, "You used to be my Scripture teacher."

I thought I might retire at 60, but I still enjoyed it, so I kept going. I'm 89 now. I see it as a place to show children that God loves them. People don't take their children to church anymore, and they don't know who God is. They need to know that God loves them, that he's still in control of the world and that they can trust him.

It's not always easy, of course. Ross got dementia in 2014. We celebrated his 90th birthday and then he died peacefully at home in 2017. Then, two years ago, I was diagnosed with macular degeneration, which got worse. I couldn't see well enough to drive, so a friend helped me and drove me to Scripture classes. I kept teaching, and the children prayed for me. I was able to get injections and my eyes slowly got better. One of the little boys said, "Jesus can still heal today!"

Now, I can see again and drive again. I'm still living in the house Ross built for me on the farm. I'm still teaching Scripture! One of my favourite verses is from Isaiah 40:31. I hold on to

> it whenever I get tired: "but those who hope in the LORD will renew their strength. They will soar on wings like eagles …"
>
> It's true! I didn't get a chance to go to Africa, but I know God has a plan for our lives. It might be different to what we think, but it's always good … and I'd like to keep teaching Scripture for as long as I can.'

For me, meeting Coral was an absolute delight. She invited me into her home in Perthville, which Ross built in 1957. We drank tea in her kitchen, surrounded by the fireplace, cupboards and furniture that he built 65 years earlier. As well as sharing her wonderful story of faith with me, she shared her gorgeous smile, which seemed to radiate from her heart of thankfulness to Jesus. I especially loved Coral's understanding of being on mission back in the 1950s – that serving Jesus could happen equally at the local garage, on the farm, at school or in Africa. And it did happen. Coral has poured out her gifts her whole life. She has been teaching Scripture for 46 years, serving the children at church and the local school and pointing them to Jesus. Even when she wasn't able to drive, her lovely friend drove her to school so that she could keep teaching and loving the children.

Thank God for gracious, servant-hearted people like Coral! I love her example of continuing to serve as long as she is able. She knows that she could retire, but she also knows that she doesn't have to. She understands that it's God who will continue to give her the passion, ability and strength to teach the children. May the children in Perthville continue to look to Jesus! May we each also continue to look to God for direction and clarity as we humbly respond to his love and seek to use the gifts he's poured out on each of us for his glory and honour. May we each continue to realise that the best way to reach the world for Jesus is to look more and more like Jesus. *Lord, we thank you for these stories, and we pray that you would keep doing your good work in our hearts as we look to you each day. Help us to love the people in front of us, in the places you have allowed us to be.*

9
At every age

I'd like us to pause for a minute and spend a chapter thinking about our different stages of life and how God works in unique ways through the decades. After writing 300 faith stories, I reread them all – not only to appreciate and enjoy them but also to pause and reflect on their contents. There were many surprising aspects. I realised that the interviewees came from 33 different countries across six continents, and represented every age bracket and a wide variety of backgrounds. No wonder I found it fascinating!

Interestingly, of the 300 stories, roughly 18% of people, like Christine and Caroline, said they had known Jesus since childhood. Another 30%, including Corey, Jodi, Karen and Lily, described experiences in their late teens that led to trusting in Jesus as their Lord and Saviour. Another large group (about 29%) came to faith in Jesus in their 20s. This group included Scott, Edgar, Tim, Badawi, Melissa, Ray, Louise and Shaun, who described profound questions and searching during those years that led them to investigate the claims of Jesus. The remaining 23% made decisions to follow Jesus between their 30s and 80s, such as Norm, Russ, Kaz, Geoff, Andrew, Alan, Roseamanda, Brenda and Angelina.

I found the mid-to-late 20-year-olds particularly interesting. Many of them were asking profound existential questions about life, meaning and purpose. Some had faced family issues or illnesses that prompted their questions, while others had no major problems but still found themselves searching for answers. Interestingly, in the following decade, a proportion of the 30-year-olds mentioned being drawn to Jesus at the turning point of having their own children. They suddenly wondered about the values they would teach them. Another group, later in life, had achieved many of their life goals but still felt unsatisfied.

I will share some more examples from each of these age groups in this chapter so we can observe and think about the trends. Perhaps after reading this book, you might like to run a survey with your Christian friends at church or at Bible study. At what ages did they first respond to Jesus? Did they experience deep questions or unravelling during the period preceding their decision to submit to Jesus as Lord? Were they aware of the influence of friends and relatives at that time? Do they remember reading the Bible for the first time or experiencing a powerful move of the Holy Spirit, convincing them of the truth? If you discover anything interesting, I'd love to hear from you! Please send me an email or a message and add your insights to this conversation.

In the meantime, I'd love to introduce you to two ladies who came to faith in Jesus in their 20s. The first is **Bridget**, whom we met through mutual friends.

> 'After finishing high school in Surrey (UK), I took a gap year. I went to New York City and worked as a nanny. Back then, I was always looking for meaning in life, and I thought that travel might be the way. After NYC, I studied in Yorkshire, and then I got a job in Papua New Guinea as a chef. I was still looking for

meaning and purpose, but I didn't know where it was. After my time in PNG, I applied for residency in Australia, and I found work as a diet technician at a large Sydney hospital.

Early on in my time there, I became friends with a girl called Alison. One day she said, "I don't know if you've ever thought about God …"

Presumably, she thought that I hadn't, by the way I described my expat lifestyle in PNG! I said to her, "Well, actually, I have been thinking about life and death and meaning, quite a lot."

While I'd been in PNG, I'd actually had a scuba diving accident and nearly drowned. When I was alone in the ocean, I cried out, "If there is a God, save me!" He did, physically, at the time.

Also, prior to the conversation with Alison, I'd been on a bus and overheard some older ladies talking about their friend who had recently died. They really cared for him. I immediately thought, well, where is he now? What is this all about? Why do we live? Why do we die? What's the point of these feelings of love and friendship, if it comes to nothing and we rot in the ground?

So, when Alison asked me that question and invited me to church, I said, "Okay, I'll come."

It was probably the most conservative church in all of Sydney. The sermon was long, the seat was hard, the ladies wore hats, and they sang psalms. But I looked around me and the people didn't seem gullible. They were listening. I thought there might be something in it. I was fascinated. I kept going to church.

> One day, the pastor spoke on Matthew 7:13–14: "Enter through the narrow gate. For wide is the gate and broad is the road that leads to destruction, and many enter through it. But small is the gate and narrow the road that leads to life, and only a few find it."
>
> I realised there was a way to life through Jesus! God was inviting me! Jesus was the way. Also, it was a bit like trying to go through a turnstile with your backpack on. The bag keeps getting caught … but you can take it off. It was amazing. I could lay my burdens and sin down. I had to lay them down. There was hope! It was a narrow way, but it was better by far. God was offering me life for now and forever.
>
> That was 30 years ago now. I stayed in Australia, which was hard for my family in the UK. For years, I had an ongoing burden to share my faith with them. Amazingly, though, my brother got saved a few years ago. He changed dramatically, and he insisted that the rest of the family look into the claims of Jesus. He died two years after that from cancer. It showed me that God doesn't work in the way we expect. Looking back, I also find it amazing that God took me all the way to Australia and saved me here. He answered my cry in the ocean in PNG – spiritually as well as physically. And he showed me that his plan is always right. I found my ultimate answers in God himself, who wonderfully saves us from suffering and death.'

I really appreciate Bridget's story, including her description of the church she visited that she thought was the most conservative in Sydney – full of hats and hard pews. And yet God worked in her heart,

9. At every age

partly because she saw the believers around her were genuinely listening, and she concluded something significant must be happening. I also valued Bridget's honest descriptions of her thought life and questions in her 20s. She was hungry for meaning and purpose, longing to understand life, death, love, friendship and the point of it all. She decided travel might be the answer, so she spent time in New York City, Yorkshire and Papua New Guinea before arriving in Sydney. The travel hadn't answered her questions, which continued unabated, although she did cry out to God in the ocean when her life was in danger. And then she heard about Jesus, who had truly saved her.

It makes me think about people in their 20s, in general. The societies we live in are rapidly changing. The distractions, technological advances and styles of communication are now vastly different from what they were a few decades ago. But at the heart of it, I think there is something unique about a person in their 20s – the big questions they tend to ask and the answers they long for. Let's meet one more person who came to faith at that same stage of life. In some ways, **Agnes** journey is the opposite of Bridget's. She began life in Hobart and now lives in London. However, it was coming to know Jesus that changed her life and her questions.

> "I moved from Hobart to Sydney in my early 20s to work in publishing. It was my first real job, as an editor in a legal publishing firm, and I loved it.
>
> I'd always wanted to work with books and ideas, so it felt like a step in the right direction. I was getting trained and developing skills. But over time, I began to question. Even with my dream job, I didn't feel like it was enough. There had to be

more to life than getting up, going to work, coming home and doing it all over again the next day.

One lunchtime, I went out and bought a book on Buddhism. I already owned New Age books and self-help books. That afternoon, my boss walked past my desk, and she saw me with the Buddhist text.

She said, "That's interesting. I've seen lots of books on your desk, a great variety, but I don't see a Christian book on your desk. Is there a reason for that?"

It was a good question. If I was truly an open-minded person, why didn't I have a Christian book in my pile? Then my boss said that her church was running a new Bible study. Did I want to come?

I went with her every week. She made it very easy. Sometimes we had dinner together before she drove me to the group. Coming from a Catholic background, I realised during that time that I wasn't well-taught in the Bible – we hadn't been encouraged to read it for ourselves. But during the Bible study, God revealed himself to me.

Everything was brought into sharp focus – my understanding of human sin, my need to repent before God and the reason why Jesus died in the first place. It felt like someone gave me the right prescription glasses, and I could suddenly see my fallen nature before God … and how incredibly he loved me.

Being the recipient of that kind of love was life-transforming, but it was also a long process. I started going to church, and I felt like I was being constantly prodded by the Holy Spirit – all my faults revealed. It took me a while to break free from my past, universalist thinking. My family believed that it was works that got you into heaven, so any system of works could be true. One kind of work was no different to another.

Then I read the words of Jesus: "I am the way and the truth and the life. No one comes to the Father except through me" (John 14:6).

Could this be true? Was Jesus the only way? I also really struggled with the concepts of predestination and the sovereignty of God. I almost walked away, but I remember praying one day, "God, I don't understand this – why you choose some people and not others – but please help me to keep trusting you and loving you, even when I don't understand."

And God in his goodness answered that prayer. It was a long process, but these days, I'm working for London City Mission. I gather stories from parts of London where life can be bleak, amongst desperate situations. But every day I see God's goodness. I see people respond to the gospel and the redeeming love of Jesus. It's amazing!'

Agnes's story is another example of God's work in our lives over long periods. In her 20s, Agnes was working in her dream job but felt full of questions. She felt there had to be more to life than this! She agreed with her employer that if she was genuinely searching for answers, she should include the Bible in her search. As she studied the Bible, God revealed himself to Agnes in a transformative way through Christ. This deeply changed her life, but some of her questions remained and God provided the answers slowly.

I think this is also a very common experience. Most of us spend our entire lives wrestling with new questions. For me, in my 50s, I'm now finding that the things I am bringing to God are very different from the questions of my 20s. But in all of it, I know that God is present. I can trust him with my different questions. I especially love the reminder in Philippians 4. Just before Paul exhorted the church in Philippi to 'not be anxious about anything', he wrote four words: 'The Lord is near' (vv. 5–6).

May each of us gain a new understanding of this truth today: the Lord is near to us. Even as we continue to have many questions and uncertainties, we can bring them to God. In all circumstances, the Lord is near. Let us also pray for the 20-year-olds in our lives, who often seem full of questions and struggles. May they bring their questions to God, and may he reveal himself to them in remarkable and surprising ways.

§

Of the 300 people I interviewed, 33 of them said they came to faith in Jesus in their 30s, including Bec and Memo. I think it's another interesting life stage. Often, people in their 30s are reasonably settled with their life partner, and sometimes they've begun a family of their own. It can be a very busy time. In listening to all these stories, though, I noticed that some of the questions became more focused during the 30s. Instead of the broad-ranging, existential questions about why we're here and what the point of it all is, the questions seemed to narrow down to the specifics of life in front of them. In many cases, for example, I heard the same repeated themes: How shall I raise my children? What values or belief systems do I hold on to? Our friend **Angela** is a lovely example of someone who wrestled with those exact questions.

> 'I grew up in a Catholic family. I prayed as a child, but there was no relationship with Jesus. And I had questions. For example, why did God make Adam and Eve, knowing that they were going to sin?
>
> One day, we had a new priest at our school. He gave a talk and then asked if we had any questions. I put up my hand and said, "Do you ever have any doubts?"
>
> He was furious with me. He said I'd committed a blasphemy. I just wanted to know. Perhaps doubts were normal? But he was very angry with me ... and as a result, I turned away from the Catholic faith. I decided it was all bunkum, and I became an agnostic.
>
> I remember feeling very much in control of my life in my 20s. I was strong and capable. I trained as a midwife, and I enjoyed my job. At 22, I moved in with my boyfriend, Warren, and after six years, we decided to get married.
>
> Then I had a breakdown. I was 28, and I got really sick with a virus. Afterwards, I had post-viral depression. It was very debilitating. I had psychotic episodes, and I couldn't tell what was real or truthful anymore. It was like living in a nightmare. I went to St John of God for five weeks. They eventually gave me shock therapy, which gave my mind a break.
>
> At one point, Warren came to see me in hospital, and I said we should call our engagement off. I gave him back the ring, and

I said, "You can't marry a madwoman!" I didn't want to be a burden on him.

Within six months, though, I did recover, and we got married, and I fell pregnant almost immediately. That brought on more questions. Who is actually in control? If I'm not in control, then who is? How are we going to raise this child? What are we going to base our family life on? What are we going to teach our children?

I suddenly wanted to go to church. It seemed completely bizarre, but I think it was because of knowing Warren's family. His parents were a lovely Christian couple who lived in Boggabri, in country New South Wales. We would go and visit them, and I could see how gentle they were with each other. They really cared for each other. And they would bow their heads before mealtimes. Their faith looked very genuine. It was quite different to my family background, and I suddenly really wanted what they had.

So, Warren and I went to church. We chose the Presbyterian church on the main street because it was an old stone building and it looked nice. At first, we would sit up the back and then run off. But after our daughter was born, I knew she was a gift from God. By then, I had seen hundreds of births (as a midwife), but I'd never really seen God's hand in creation. And then she was born, and everything was different. We knew we wanted to get her baptised. The minister suggested that we do a course called Christianity Explained. We both agreed, and as part of the course, we read John's Gospel. That's when it became obvious to me. Jesus was in charge! He

> had absolute authority over the Earth. I accepted it immediately and so did Warren. We decided together that we wanted to base our family life on Jesus. We kept going to the church!
>
> Looking back now, I want to say to people, "Give Jesus a go." I know that I don't have all the answers, but I know the One who does. I still have questions, but it's okay because I know Jesus and I can trust him. I love the truth in John 1: "In the beginning was the Word, and the Word was with God, and the Word was God" (v. 1). It reminds me every day that I'm not in charge, and that I can trust the One who is!'

Angela's story is honest and compelling, isn't it? She said she was doing fine in her 20s, feeling strong and capable, and then suddenly, she wasn't. Her mind fell apart, and she needed hospitalisation. After her recovery, having a child brought on more specific questions in her early 30s. Who is really in control? Is God's hand in the creation of our children? How should we raise them? I love that Angela and Warren were drawn back to the church and came to know Jesus through reading the Bible.

For those of us, like Angela, who enjoy the feeling of being in control yet suspect that we aren't, it's wonderful that the Bible has the answers. The truth of John 1 is so glorious. God formed all things, and he sustains all things – all of time, all of space, all of humanity. Even the most capable of us will fall apart at some point. It's part of being human – finite and weak. Yet, today, we can know the One who has the answers. We can know the One who is in control. We can trust him with all our questions.

As a parent of young adults who bring their friends home and watch us say grace, I love that in her time of crisis, Angela remembered the quiet gentleness of her believing in-laws. She wanted what they had. She sensed they had a genuine faith in Jesus. This is very encouraging! It brings us to God in prayer, aware of his glorious sovereignty, and with a desire to lay our lives down again, knowing that he holds all things in his capable hands. We can't fully comprehend it, but it's marvellous to us.

§

I'd love to share one more example of a person coming to faith in Jesus in their 30s. Like Angela, **Lisa** described parenting as being the wake-up call she needed.

> 'I was raised in a typical Aussie Catholic fashion. I got to the age of 16 and was given a choice to keep going to church or to sleep in on a Sunday. It was a no-brainer for me. I slept in … for about a decade!
>
> When I was 22, my mum died. She was only 40. Whatever relationship I had with God before that was absolutely severed. The thought of a God who would take my mother away was outrageous to me. I became very hard-hearted towards God, and very angry. I wasn't in a good place, mentally. For about five years, I drank too much alcohol as a coping mechanism.
>
> At the same time, my career was really taking off. I was involved in the travel industry, quite successfully – travelling the world, wanting for nothing. It was a hedonistic and self-obsessed lifestyle!

Then I had my daughter, Ruby, at age 31. She was an unexpected joy! Parenting literally swept me off my feet. I was besotted with her. It was also a wake-up call. I wanted to do a good job as Ruby's mum. But what values would we live by? How would we raise this child?

Weirdly, I also had an overwhelming desire to have Ruby baptised. It was a strange thought, but I knew there was a little Anglican church around the corner in our part of Melbourne, so I went and spoke with the minister. In my mind, I thought I would go in, get Ruby baptised, and then go home again and never return to church again. That was my intention.

But the minister said they were running the Alpha (evangelistic) course. He suggested that I come. I didn't know what it was, but I felt morally obliged. If they were going to baptise Ruby, then I should do the course, whatever it was. I didn't know it was a 10-week commitment!

But I went to the course, and it was really good. The people were very friendly. Everyone was so warm and kind. One of the ladies offered to babysit Ruby so I could come. And I found the course content very compelling. Every week, I'd go along and have all my questions answered! On the final week of the course, we went away for the weekend, and we learnt about the Holy Spirit. I didn't know anything about the Holy Spirit.

It was amazing. It was unbelievable the way God worked in me that weekend to reveal himself to me. I experienced all the emotions. I understood that God was real! He had come to make himself known. The significance of Jesus' death and forgiveness of sins came later, but that weekend, it was all about an encounter with God. It was highly personal, and it changed everything for me. I turned into a complete Jesus freak!

I started going to church and Bible study all the time. I was hungry to know more of God and Jesus. I've been like that ever since! Twenty-three years later, I'm still involved in Alpha! I also started a new business called Mission Travel. We specialised in sending people all over the world with their Christian mission agencies, organising their flights and visas and documents. It was great! Along the way, I also started doing Holy Land Tours ... and that's mostly what I'm doing now. I think it's a wonderful form of Christian discipleship, transforming the way people read the Bible. It's fabulous!

Now, as I look back, I realise that God took me – a high-flying, ratbag party girl – and turned me into a disciple of Jesus. He's even brought fruit from my life! I especially love the verse in John 15:5: "I am the vine; you are the branches. If you remain in me and I in you, you will bear much fruit; apart from me you can do nothing."

For 30 years, without God, I could do nothing at all, but now everything is different. If I remain in God, he will produce much fruit. That's amazing!'

I love Lisa's enthusiasm and delight in knowing Jesus! She is such a transformed person, constantly committed to using her gifts to serve others and further the kingdom. Like Angela, her journey began with the birth of her first child and her desire to get Ruby baptised. This is a good reminder for those of us who often spend time with young families – whether it's in our workplaces, extended families or local communities. We might notice a new season of openness to God following the wonder and gift of new birth. This openness can bring much fruit, drawing the person into a new and living relationship with our glorious Creator God through the Lord Jesus.

§

Another stage of life, often occurring in the late 40s and 50s, can bring a new sense of emptiness. By this time, a person may have achieved their career goals or long-held dreams. Their families may be growing up, leaving them with more time to think. They may also be facing the truth that more than half their life is over, leading to questions about the point of it all or a new openness to the things of God. **Ian** is an example. For him, it wasn't necessarily that his questions changed; it was more that he understood the compelling reality of God at age 50, after decades of hearing snippets of truth.

> 'As a young person, I was into sports cars, sailing and going to the pub on Friday nights. It was pretty harmless, but it was also meaningless. I had no church background. When I was 15, a school friend was being confirmed at his church, and he asked me to come with him. I went to the classes, but I can't claim I understood what I was doing. It was more of a social thing. Afterwards, I had some involvement with that church for a short time, but the message didn't make any impact at all. It was partly because I had no concept that I was a sinner or that I needed anything at all.
>
> In 1979, I was 36 and working in corporate finance. For some reason, I was inspired to go and hear Billy Graham speak at

Randwick. No one invited me to go; it was just a feeling I had. Afterwards, when they invited people to come forward, I had a compulsion to respond. I sensed it was important, but I failed to have a true understanding. Later, I had some follow-up from the local church, and I attended that church for a year, but I still lacked understanding, and after a year I ceased attending. I still hadn't read the Bible.

In 1991, I was working with a friend who was a well-known stockbroker and commercial analyst. He gave me and others in the office a small Gideons Bible for Christmas. I accepted it gratefully. I knew it was important, and I intended to read it, but I didn't get around to it for a few years. My weekends were taken up with sporting activities – sailing, running, cycling and squash.

In early 1993, I woke up on a Sunday morning at 6 am and was deciding what to do for the day. I heard an inner voice saying, "What about coming to church?"

I said, "What? I can't do that. Don't be ridiculous."

That morning, I lay in bed wrestling with the voice until it was too late to go to church. At 8 am, the voice stopped.

The same thing happened the next Sunday and the next and the next – the same inner voice. It was not a threatening voice. It was so real and encouraging. On the fourth Sunday, I said, "All right, I'll go."

I went to church at 8 am, but the service had already started at 7:45 am. I didn't enter and I left, but I made a promise that I would go to church the next week at the correct time.

The next week I went to church. I was 50 by then. It was very emotional. I just felt overwhelmed. I knew it was where I should be. The Lord called me to church, and then he called me to faith in Jesus. At home, I started to read the Gideons Bible, from beginning to end. It was the most inspiring read. I knew I had to find out more about Jesus.

The minister invited me to a growth group. The first time I went, I realised I knew absolutely nothing. I bought myself a bigger Bible, and later I started doing a preliminary theological course through Moore College. I found it enlightening – truths I'd never thought of before, mainly that I was a sinner, fallen short of the glory of God. The only thing I could do was put my faith in the Lord Jesus, and I would be clothed in his righteousness!

It changed me in every way. At work, I began to remove myself from dollar-motivated behaviour and the colourful language people used to impress each other. After I retired, I moved from Sydney to Oberon to try my hand at farming. The Lord led me to a little local Anglican church, and after a few years, I became a lay preacher!

The key verse for me has always been John 14:6: "Jesus answered, 'I am the way and the truth and the life. No one comes to the Father except through me.'"

When we understand our deepest needs, we realise that Jesus is the only way!'

Isn't that wonderful? The Holy Spirit was quietly persistent in Ian's life for decades until that Sunday morning in 1993, when he heard an inner voice telling him to go to church at age 50. I love how Ian describes the voice as real and encouraging, not threatening at all. Naturally, he wanted to respond to it! As Ian came to understand the gospel, he saw great changes in his life, both in his world of finance and then later as a lay preacher. Having met Ian more recently, I'm very thankful for his quiet humility and openness to service.

Ian's story also makes me more aware and expectant. It reminds me that God can suddenly move in a person's life, no matter what their age or how settled they seem in their current routines. May we each be encouraged by that truth today and each look to God with fresh expectancy and prayerful dependence. Jesus is the way, the truth and the life!

§

Lastly, in this chapter, I'd love you to meet **Joyce**. She told me in her delighted, excitable voice that she came to know Jesus for the first time at age 80.

> 'I went to church when I was younger. I was confirmed at age 16. But I didn't remain in the church. I married my husband, David, and we were building our house. We had three children. David was an estimator for a building company, so he worked on the weekends. I suppose you could say that life got busy.
>
> Then our three children became teenagers and two of them went off to Young Life camps. They both became Christians. Then the eldest became a Christian when he was about 25. All three of them went into the ministry. They became pastors and

ministers, and so did their wives and husbands. They brought their children up to be Christians.

Because of that, they were always asking me to come to church. They were always telling me that they were praying for me. But I resisted. I was really good at resisting!

Then, when I was 79, David became unwell. He was diagnosed with a brain tumour and the next week he had an operation. We moved from the Central Coast to a retirement village in Berry, New South Wales. We got a spot straight away, and I sort of felt I was being looked after. I started going to the knitting group at church. It was called Knit with Love, and it met on Fridays. One of my Christian friends went there as well, and she said they were all praying for me.

I tell you, it's very hard to resist that amount of praying!

At the time, I was searching. I knew there was something missing in my life. David had passed away, and I was lonely. I said to my friend, "How do you become a Christian?" and she said, "You just pray to God."

At the time, a local church was having an adult baptism at the beach. So, I said, "I can do that by myself." I went down to the local pool by myself, and I prayed to God with the Lord's Prayer and the Apostles' Creed. There was nobody else there.

And I was zapped by the Holy Spirit! I felt great joy and euphoria. I was overcome by a strong perfumed aura, and I've had it many times since. It's given me great calmness and comfort at different times. I felt completely set free! You would never believe what the Holy Spirit has done in my life since I turned 80!

> Then I thought, I suppose I can't be a Christian and not go to church. So, I started going to church. These days, I'm working on my knowledge of the Bible with daily reading and study. I have experienced Christ near me. I'm 82 and a half, so it's been two-and-a-half years since I came to Christ. I hope that my life is an example to other people. I hope I can prove it's never too late to come to Christ!
>
> At the moment, I'm reading Isaiah 41: "I have chosen you and have not rejected you. So do not fear, for I am with you; do not be dismayed, for I am your God" (vv. 9–10).
>
> God has chosen us, and he holds us in his hands. That's pretty amazing! Recently I was at my granddaughter's engagement party, and one of my friends said to me, "You look different. You're glowing with happiness. What's happened? Have you become a Christian?" I said, "Yes!" All my family members have rejoiced in my conversion. And I say to everyone, "It's never too late to come to Christ!"'

I love Joyce's story. I first met her at a large church lunch in Berry, not long after she became a Christian. We were sitting at the same table, both eating chicken and cucumber sandwiches, and she was bubbling over with excitement and joy about her new faith in the Lord Jesus. She was 81. It's never too late to turn to Jesus!

I also smiled when she said it was very hard to resist that amount of prayer. Congratulations to her family members for praying and never giving up. It's wonderful that they noticed Joyce looked different, glowing with happiness. I especially loved her story of going off to the pool all on her own and getting zapped by the Holy Spirit.

9. At every age

Sometimes, it's easy to think, as the persistent praying family members, that we have to do all the right things or say the right things. Then God just zaps the person we love in his way and timing! It makes me thankful for knitting clubs, Christian friends, and honest questions during times of loneliness. May the Holy Spirit continue to work in the lives of our loved ones in his good timing. May we remember that it's never too late to come to Christ while we each have breath! And may God help us to keep praying and keep expecting his answers in the lives of the people we love, in his good timing.

10
Faithfulness to the end

As I was gathering 300 faith stories, I noticed that I was repeatedly being drawn to the stories of older Christians, often in their 80s or 90s. Some of them, like Joyce, had recently come to faith in Jesus, but many of them, like Coral, had lived long years of faithfulness to him. I found myself increasingly captivated by their rich perspectives. As I listened and typed, I wanted to slow down and soak in their hard-earned wisdom. I wanted to learn from them and perhaps gain glimpses into that next season of life.

Darren and I are now in our mid-to-late 50s. As I mentioned in chapter 8, we recently moved from our home in the Blue Mountains to a small town in rural New South Wales. Before our move, all of our three sons left home, and we became empty nesters. Everything suddenly seemed very quiet! It was reminiscent of when we moved back from Nepal to the Blue Mountains in 2006, except this time, the quietness lasted much longer than six hours each day! At the same time, Darren and I felt led by God to move west to support smaller rural churches and communities. So, we bought an old house on four acres on the outskirts of a small town in the Central West of New South Wales and made the move.

It's been mostly wonderful. Our new home is surrounded by daffodils in the springtime, snow in the winter and woolly lambs all year round. We've made some lovely new friends at the local church, and

10. Faithfulness to the end

we have plans to take Faith Stories on the road in 2024 and beyond, to surrounding towns and villages in rural Australia. We're hoping to jump in a campervan and arrive at outback churches, set up camp nearby, make some friends ... and then pop out the awning and a couple of chairs, a pot of tea and a lovely invitation: 'Would you like to share your story?'

However, we're also very aware that we're getting older. We have less time left and less energy than back in 1993 when we bought a one-way ticket and moved to Nepal. We creak a bit when we get up in the mornings, and we have trouble remembering names and other things we used to know. We're in a different stage of life! Hopefully, though, alongside the increase in creaking and forgetfulness, we're also a bit softer, wiser and more expectant. There is much beauty in being able to look back and draw from those rich wells of experience in a lifelong walk with Jesus. The lesson for me is not to compare myself with a previous, more energetic version of myself but to look around and see the opportunities present today, with the same calling to love each other as Jesus loved us and the promise of his enabling in everything.

One of the things that has really helped me is hearing the stories of older Christians – those who have gone ahead of me. They have so much encouragement and godly wisdom to share. Of the 300 people I interviewed, 39 were in their 80s and 90s. Seven of the 39 have now died and gone to be with their Lord. I'm so thankful for each of them. I've decided to close this book with a chapter dedicated to all the older men and women who are in their last chapter of serving Jesus here on earth. May we be blessed by reading their stories.

I'm going to start with **Marg**. She would say, of course, that she's lived a very quiet, ordinary life and hasn't got much to say. But Marg has poured out her days, quietly, in response to Jesus, amongst her family and community members. She is also the mother of my dear friend, who invited me to the Christian group on that Friday lunchtime back in 1980. Marg is the reason that I first experienced what it means to love Jesus in the ordinary day-to-day moments of family life. I'm sure you will love her as well.

> 'My dad was a Presbyterian minister from Scotland. He and Eric Liddell were in the same Bible classes. They were friends. Dad and a few others came out to Australia in 1930 to help the Presbyterian Church in Queensland. He had a very simple faith, but it had a profound impact on me. He met my mum in one of the churches, and they married and had three kids. We moved around a bit as a family because he was the minister in five different places. It was a poor but loving home, and I heard plenty of Scripture. Dad kept saying that we were to love God and love people. That was it. He was strict as well, and I was a bit of a cheeky monster. But he kept saying the same thing … and after he died, I put his sermons in a basket, and I kept them.
>
> I feel like I haven't done anything out of the ordinary. I'm 80 now, and I've always been part of a church. For the last 50 years, I've been part of our church in Sydney. I love that our doors are always open. We try to love people and not judge them. I help with the playgroup and also a group that supports the older women. Twice a year, we run a flea market, and we raise about $22,000. We give it all away. We've been doing it for decades. I also trained as a teacher, and I

taught for 27 years. That was after taking 15 years off to raise our four children.

Six years ago, a beautiful friend asked me to come on her Kairos 'outside' team. It's a group that supports women who have family members or friends inside the prisons. It breaks my heart listening to their stories. We help them by inviting them as guests on weekends away, and we really listen to them and accept them. We all weep together. We never judge them. And every week, I make a few follow-up phone calls to keep in touch with them. I think God has taught me a lot by getting me outside my comfort zone. If only we could realise that all people are humans just like us.

I feel like I've changed in the last half of my life. I'm more relaxed now. I did have a problem with flying off the handle when the kids were little. I don't think I had enough time to immerse myself in Scripture. But recently, that's changed again. I'm finding more time. I'm becoming closer to God again. I often feel like the two disciples who were walking with Jesus on the road to Emmaus. They said, "Were not our hearts burning within us while he talked with us on the road and opened the Scriptures to us?" (Luke 24:32). That's how it's been for me. Scripture is so heartwarming!

Lately, I've also been thinking about how I can share the truth with my 11 blessings (my grandchildren). How can I tell them that loving God is the most important thing? Then, just this week, I was reminded again. We were cleaning out our house because we were about to sell it, and I found the basket of my dad's old sermons. I sat down and started reading them

> again. I've been using them as my devotional material. They're so precious! It's the same truth. Just love. Love God first, then love others. It's the way to true happiness. Maybe I'll show that to my grandchildren by keeping on doing what I'm doing ...'

As I write this, Marg is in palliative care, facing end-stage heart failure. She has loved God, her family and her community with her whole heart, every day of her life. Despite not having long to go, she continues to insist that her story is ordinary, while I maintain that it's wonderful. I especially admire how Marg has faithfully supported her local church for 50 years. It's inspiring that in her 70s, she stepped out of her comfort zone to volunteer with Kairos, supporting women who had loved ones in prison. Even though she had no prior experience in that area, she brought her heart of love and welcome, and people were blessed. Now that I'm also getting older, I realise that it's no small feat to begin new projects and ministries as we age.

Most of all, I appreciate Marg's honesty about her own walk with Jesus. She looks back on her life and sees that in her later decades, she has become more relaxed and able to spend time in the Scriptures. Immersing herself in God's word has further changed her heart's response to God, increasing her love for him and her family. May we each join Marg in her prayer for her grandchildren – and for grandchildren everywhere – that they might come to see, know and love the Lord Jesus, as Marg has done so faithfully. May our lives also bring that same faithful witness to Jesus as we follow his simplest and loveliest commandment, 'Love the Lord your God with all your heart and with all your soul and with all your strength and with all your mind; and, love your neighbour as yourself' (Luke 10:27).

10. Faithfulness to the end

§

A year ago, Darren and I were visiting one of our sons in West Wyalong, New South Wales, and we attended the local church on Christmas Day. In between the Christmas carols, the minister got up and announced that **Judith** would be leading us in prayer. In front of us, an elderly lady slowly stood up, pushed her walker up the aisle to the lectern, closed her eyes and began to pray fervently. I turned and whispered to Darren, 'I have to get her faith story!'

> 'I was born in Bundaberg, Queensland, 91 years ago. My father was a minister of religion, and we moved every three or four years. But my parents had a great capacity to love, and we were nurtured in prayer and the word of God. We were always talking to our heavenly Father, who was a natural part of our daily lives. God was especially a source of great stability during the turbulent times of World War 2, with ration books, blackout curtains and air-raid shelters. Every day we went to school with a Scripture verse in our pocket.
>
> At 19 years old, I began nursing training in a district hospital. I was the only Christian in my year, working long hours and lacking spiritual fellowship. At times I wondered where God was. In the first month, I was on night duty in a surgical ward full of motor-accident victims, in the days before seatbelts and helmets. It was horrible. I went off-duty feeling emotionally drained and thinking, 'I can't go back tomorrow.'
>
> I threw myself on my knees, and I cried out to God, "Are you real, or is it just my parents' faith? Show me, Lord; I'm sinking in the rapids."

God came to me in a quietness in my spirit, a peace I hadn't known before. He gave me a verse from Psalm 42:5: "Why, my soul, are you downcast? Why so disturbed within me? Put your hope in God, for I will yet praise him, my Saviour and my God."

The Psalm basically says – put your hope in God! That day, I put my hope in God, and I found not only a bigger, more approachable God, but I found my own identity, which lasted my whole life. It was like I was weaned from my parents' faith. And ever since then, God has been giving me psalms.

I've had many good years – working as a midwife, meeting my husband (Peter) and being blessed with four children. I was always very involved in Sunday school teaching, leading Bible studies, speaking at church events and pastoral visiting. I love people and Jesus!

But God doesn't stand still. One day I said goodbye to Peter as he went to his weekly tennis game. An hour later, I was rung to say Peter was in the ICU, having had a cardiac arrest. He was not expected to live. I was 59, and we had been planning our retirement – trips away and carefree days. I went to the hospital and spent three weeks at his bedside, with him semi-conscious before God took him home.

I remember the funeral. There were a hundred or more people there. I felt very vulnerable, especially afterwards when everyone was shaking my hand. I was weary and worn out. But that morning God gave me a psalm: "I remain confident of this: I will see the goodness of the LORD in the land of the living" (Ps 27:13).

If God hadn't been with me, I would have fainted. He was the only thing that got me through. Afterwards, I had to learn to face life on my own. Again, God's word became my stability. Every morning, God gave me a new verse from a psalm to hold on to. They spoke to my soul.

The harder test has come recently. I'm 91, and I can't do the things I used to do for God. It started when I was 86. I had to give up teaching Sunday school because I couldn't hear very well. Then I couldn't speak at church events or lead Bible studies. I couldn't do pastoral visiting. I felt very empty and unsure of myself. I remember saying to God, "Lord, I have nothing to give. I am nobody."

I think it had been subconscious spiritual pride before that. But God stripped me of it. He showed me that everything I had was in him. He reassured me that I was his child, at age 86, and he was my Father. I didn't have to prove myself. He has a deep love for nobodies! Even now, at 91, I can still pray. I can still send cards to people instead of visiting them.

As I look back over my life, I am humbled to see how long it has taken for me to learn things. But I see the hand of God in every part! And if God takes me home in the night, I'm ready! I'm looking forward to seeing the Lord!'

God has been at work in Judith's life in beautiful ways through every decade, showing her his truth, giving her psalms, enabling her ministry and comforting her in her hardest times of grief. It must have been such a terrible shock to lose her husband, Peter, when she was 59. I can't imagine the numbness and exhaustion she felt at the funeral, but God held her tight. For those of us who haven't yet stood and grieved at the funeral of our life partner, we find deep comfort in her story. We know that those days may come. Grief sits at the door and waits for all of us in different forms. But we pray that when those days do come, we will turn to God and find the same deep comfort that Judith found. We too will see the goodness of the Lord in the land of the living.

I also loved the latter part of Judith's story. She was so honest with me about her experience at age 86, when she realised that she could no longer hear well enough to lead Bible studies or make pastoral visits. For the first time, she wondered: Who am I? Am I nobody? She said it was her hardest test and yet the most profound truth of all. God has a deep love for nobodies. God said that she was his child. Everything she had was in him. And she could still pray and send cards. Since meeting Judith, I have been on the receiving end of her prayers and phone messages. I can assure you, it's a wonderful gift to pour out!

But I also acknowledge the deep struggle of growing older and losing some of our roles in ministry, communities and families. We step aside, thinking it's the right time, and then other people fill those roles. Sometimes they do it better than us, and our pride is a constant thing to be aware of.

Yet, there is also an opportunity to do business with God, as Richard described back in chapter 7. When everything is stripped away, who are we? When all our clever answers are no longer wanted, who are we? When we can no longer hear or see, who are we? When we can no longer type, speak or read the Bible, who are we?

10. Faithfulness to the end

We are children of God, loved by him. May we each absorb the deep truth of that message again today.

§

It's true that none of us know how many days we have left on earth. We don't know if we'll live to our 90s like Judith and Coral. We don't know if we'll be called home in our 50s, like Judith's husband Peter. Indeed, we don't know if Jesus will return beforehand and take us to be with him. But living with that uncertainty and the possibility of failing health and ongoing loss can be hard. Perhaps when that stage comes to each of us, we will need to surround ourselves with stories from people like **Joe**. I find his attitude to his remaining days beautiful.

> 'I'm 101, and I've still got most of my marbles. I'm weak in my body, but I can still pray. I have much to be thankful for! I first opened my heart to Jesus at a Scripture Union camp in London, when I was 17. Two years later, World War 2 broke out and I signed up for the British army. I was commissioned as a 2nd Lieutenant in 1940, and we were sent out to Peshawar, which is now Pakistan, but it was India at the time.
>
> In 1945, I was leading our company in a battle to regain a village in Burma. I'll never forget it. It was the monsoon. We were moving through pouring rain, on mules, over the hills. The Japanese were trying to escape out of Burma, and we were sent to cut them off. On 27th July, there was a battle. Snipers were firing. Eventually the Japanese withdrew ... and we walked back through the village. It was about 12 hours afterwards that I took my steel helmet off and I felt a small

scratch on the top of my head. I pulled the rubber and leather out of my helmet, and I saw two holes straight through my helmet. Two bullets had gone through, and a third bullet had ricocheted off it.

There was no booming voice from heaven, but it came into my mind, "Joe, you have no right to be alive. Give your life fully to me."

Since I was 17, I'd always tried to read my Bible, but it was hard in the army. I'd backslidden a bit, mostly praying to the Lord to stay alive. But the Lord graciously held on to me – until that battle in Burma. The bullets through my helmet felt like a wake-up call.

Afterwards, I lay in hospital for eight weeks. My legs had gone septic, and they took eight weeks to heal. But I believe it was part of God's plan. Lying there gave me time to rethink my life and my faith. The Lord had graciously saved me for a purpose. What did he want me to do?

After I got out of hospital, I went back to England, and I graduated with a theology degree from Oxford, by God's mercy. I was never a great student. After two years of serving as a curate in London, I responded to God's call to serve him in India. I knew about the needs in South-East Asia because of my time there in the war. I worked with Scripture Union there for 10 years, and it was a great opportunity for the gospel. During that time, I met my wife, Edith. We married and we had six children. We stayed in India for 22 years. It was a greatly encouraging time.

> Then in 1974, we immigrated to Canberra, with our six children in tow. God very graciously led us here. I began serving in a Canberra parish, and later in the wider region. Today, I thank God that the Lord Jesus has become increasingly real to me over all these years, even in this retirement village in lockdown due to the pandemic. I still seek to be a witness, as best I can, amongst the elderly people here. This morning, I read Matthew 21 – the lead-up to the crucifixion – the wonder of Jesus dying for us and for the sins of the whole world! And I can pray. It's the one thing we can do, as we get older. I can pray for the world, for Iran and Afghanistan, and for my family. "Keep me true, Lord Jesus!" I've got 22 grandchildren and 23 great-grandchildren now, and I pray that they all know Jesus and follow his plans for them. I also have a nice room with a view. I have much to be thankful for!'

Joe is a man who seems to be filled up with gratitude. He said it started in that village in Burma, where he knew he could so easily have died from the gunshot, and it continued for the next 80 years. In some ways, his near-death experience is similar to the other stories we've read in this book, like Allan in chapter 2 or Michael in chapter 6. Close calls with death can give us a wake-up call. Why are we alive? How are we living the days God has given us? Is our faith real, or is it merely words we recite when required? Are we following Jesus fully? For Joe, he noticed the wake-up call and responded to God's grace. He went back to England to study theology; then he served in India for 22 years and later in Canberra for 48 years. That's a lot of years! At age 101, he isn't finished yet. He is busy praying and being a witness to the other residents in his retirement home, even during lockdown. He is still following Jesus and is still amazed by God's saving plan.

This greatly encourages me. It reminds me that Jesus' invitation to all of us to follow him is not just for this week or this year. In Matthew 4:19, Jesus said, 'Come, follow me … and I will send you out to fish for people.' That command and enabling continue throughout our entire lives. We may still be seeking Jesus and following him at age 101! It makes me get down on my knees in thankfulness to God and long to pray like Joe prays. *Keep us true to you, wherever we are, Lord Jesus!*

§

Joe may be faithfully serving the Lord at age 101, but we know that many of us won't be given that same opportunity. God truly numbers our days, and we can trust him with the number. In ways we may never fathom, God may choose to call some of us to our eternal home much earlier than we expect. **Moyra**, a gorgeous and wise lady, shared her story with me a few months before she died.

> 'We lived in the Middle East for 22 years. I worked in Arabic adult literacy and teacher training. In 2007, we came home to Melbourne, and I began teaching cultural anthropology at the CMS training college and other Bible colleges.
>
> What I love most about this subject is digging into cultural themes and then exploring the biblical response. For example, what do envy, sorcery and the evil eye look like in different cultures? What does the Bible say about them, in the context of God's abundant generosity? It's a joy seeing culture and the Bible in conversation as they illuminate each other!

In the past, I think we haven't talked much about Muslim women. We get trained in Islam at Bible colleges, and it's usually done by wonderful, godly men who know nothing about Muslim women ... and so we're actually being trained in how to reach Muslim men.

Muslim women face similar issues as women in other faith systems, such as Buddhism or Hinduism. As part of our time overseas, I spent some years attending a women's program in a Muslim mosque. I realised that Muslim women are often living in a faith space that has been largely defined by male scholars – not dissimilar to women in the evangelical church in Australia!

So, for the past six years, I have been part of an organisation called When Women Speak. It's a web-based network connecting Christian women working in Muslim communities all around the world. The settings and challenges may be different (whether in Afghanistan, the Middle East or Indonesia), but the connections are wonderful. We're listening to women, and we're hearing their longing for a personal relationship with God.

At the same time, I've also been living with cancer. I was diagnosed five years ago and given five months to live. I'm surprised to be here right now! The cancer started in my lungs, with secondaries in my bones and brain. At the time, I had to step back from my work. I was about to take up some wider roles in the organisation, but stepping back has been a gift. In fact, cancer has been a really precious journey, pulling me back and focusing me more and more on Jesus. I've discovered his presence more constantly and more deeply.

> Then, a couple of months ago, I went back to my doctor for my regular check-up, not expecting any developments. But it was the opposite. My doctor said the drug therapy was no longer working, and the cancer has now spread to my liver. I'm on chemo, and I know I'm closer to the end.
>
> Recently, I've been going through all the psalms again. In fact, moments before I saw my oncologist, I happened to be reading Psalm 73:26: "My flesh and my heart may fail, but God is the strength of my heart and my portion forever."
>
> I know that my body will fail, but I don't have to worry. God remains the strength of my life and my portion forever; it doesn't depend on me or my own strength. When so much is taken away, what remains the most important thing? It's still to seek Jesus, to be known by him and to know his love for each one of us.'

Not long before Moyra died, her wonderful book was published. It's called *Islam and Women: Hagar's Heritage*. It's a rich text, born from the depths of her heart and decades of work and conversations with Muslim women. Throughout Moyra's life and writing, she has longed to remind people that God truly cares for women, answers their cries and honours them. God hears them. It's a deeply needed message today.

Talking to Moyra not long before she passed away was so precious to me. I found it profound that she was learning that same truth at deeper and deeper levels. She was very near the end of her time on earth, yet she said she was increasingly aware of the presence of Jesus. She was leaning into God as her strength and portion forever. She was testifying to the truth that God truly answers her cries and honours her. She was loving her family. She even said she was thankful for her cancer journey. There was a beautiful, genuine synergy that encouraged me. For all of us, may the words we speak or choose to put into print throughout our lifetimes also be the words that we live by, right to the end, even when our health may fail. Even then, may Jesus truly be the strength of our lives. We know that our bodies will fail and our spirits will grow weak, yet Jesus remains the same. *Lord, please help us to remember the most important thing, every day, and even at the end – to seek you and be known by you.*

§

Do you remember Ian's story in chapter 9? Ian explained to me that he came to faith in Jesus at age 50, in part because his stockbroker colleague gave him a Gideons Bible. After Ian's faith story was published online, I received a message from a man in Sydney by the name of Scott. Scott wanted to know if the stockbroker in Ian's story was his Uncle **Russell**. I did some investigations, and it turned out to be the case. So then, of course, I asked if Russell would like to share *his* faith story with me. Scott explained that Russell was currently in hospital, but yes, he said that Russell would love to speak to me over the phone. This is what Russell shared.

> 'I am in hospital at the moment, awaiting an operation for pancreatic cancer. But it's an opportunity. I dwell on the Scriptures, and I talk to the nurses. Most of them know nothing about Jesus. They're young, and they're thinking about their career paths. They're not thinking about the life hereafter at

all, even though they see people going there all the time. They haven't given that life even a thought.

I was born in 1938 ... and at age nine, I went to a Christian boarding school in Armidale. I started to have a belief in Jesus from that point. We had a wonderful chaplain who had been in the trenches in World War 1 and seen a lot of life. I admired him. We had prayers every morning and a lot of Christians around us. I think the truth of the gospel just attached itself to me. When I left school, I made a point of attending church every week. That's what kept me going – being perpetually surrounded by the gospel. And I married a lovely Christian girl, Margot. We've been together for more than 60 years!

But my moment of change came when I joined the Gideons in 1984. I became part of a world where we saw the Lord at work. I joined others committed to prayer, giving out Bibles and being a Christian witness. We would meet weekly to be fortified in our faith ... and we saw the Lord use us. We received thousands of letters, all of them reminding us that when people read the Scriptures, it changes lives. Every time, of course, we gave out a Bible, we didn't know what the Lord would do. We always scattered them in faith, trusting that his word wouldn't return void, as it says in Isaiah 55:11.

Over the years, I must have given out hundreds of Bibles. I generally give them out in appreciation of people. I say thank you to the person for a favour they've done for me, and then I tell them the Bible is a small token of my appreciation. In 40 years, I've only ever had one knockback.

10. Faithfulness to the end

One year, in 1992, I gave a Bible to a friend of mine at work, Ian. We were in our 50s, working in stockbroking. At first, he said he didn't need it, but then he took it … and a few years later, he wrote to me to say he'd had strange promptings to go to church. Then he read the Bible and came to Christ. He asked if could he have another Bible. He went on to Bible college and became a lay preacher. It was very encouraging!

In stockbroking, it's all about the dollars. How do you make more dollars? But Christians are needed in every sphere of life, including finance. I stayed in broking from age 23 to 81. I enjoyed it. It was a career and an opportunity to share the gospel. Of course, the Lord breaks down barriers without any trouble at all!

Right now, as I said, I'm in hospital. While I've been here, I've given out 13 Bibles to different nurses. I find it's also an opportunity to tell them I'm not afraid. I'm going into major surgery, but I'm not afraid. Margot and I are both content with whatever the outcome is. If I survive this cancer, that will be okay. If I don't survive it, that will also be okay. I know where I'm going! The nurses tend to be surprised. It's not what they normally hear!

I think that wherever we are, there are avenues for ministry. And it's never about me. The Lord is the one who works! This week, I've been reading Zephaniah 3:17: "The LORD your God is with you, the Mighty Warrior who saves. He will take great delight in you; in his love he will no longer rebuke you, but will rejoice over you with singing."

> It's always wonderful to dwell in the Scriptures ... and the truth is that God saves us. He rejoices over us with singing!'

It's an encouraging testimony, isn't it? Three weeks after our phone conversation, Scott contacted me again to say that Russell had passed away peacefully and had gone to be with Jesus. Scott also mentioned that Russell had very much appreciated being able to share his faith story with us while he could. He was thankful.

I personally love the way Russell described his journey of faith. The truth of the gospel just attached itself to him. Then, in his 40s, he became involved with Gideons, and he saw God at work daily. He realised that Scripture changes lives! Russell gave out hundreds of Bibles as thank-you gifts, and almost always, people received them without refusal, including Ian, who later came to faith. As a side note, after Ian came to faith in 1993, the two friends reconnected briefly. Russell heard that Ian had become a lay preacher, but after some years, they lost contact again. Late last year, when both their faith stories were shared online by *Eternity News*, they reconnected and chatted on the phone for the first time in 25 years. They were both very encouraged. One week later, Russell died. It's true that God's timing and ways are extraordinary.

I also find it encouraging that being in hospital at the end of Russell's life didn't change his focus. He longed to share the truths of Jesus with everyone he could, especially the hospital staff who weren't thinking about the life hereafter. It reminds me of Caroline's story back in chapter 6. She said she was working at a hospital as a nurse and noticed that when people died with a faith in God, there was a peace. For others, they would sometimes die in terror, which made her wonder. It also makes me wonder whether the staff members who were caring for Russell at the time noticed the peace he described. Did it make them think and question? We don't know. Certainly, Russell had a God-given peace and joy in going home. He was so thankful for a rich life of service, and he kept telling me that it was about the Lord, not him. May we each draw encouragement from Russell's life, remembering that the Lord our God is with us in everything. He takes great delight in us. He rejoices over us with singing.

§

It has indeed been a great privilege for me to spend time with people who know that their days are numbered. It's almost as if, for them, everything comes into sharp focus. The important things shine more. Their words carry more weight. Their perspective shifts, and their eyes seem to see Jesus more clearly. I remember when we were living in Nepal in 2005, I spent a lot of time with my friend Jalpa, who was the same age as me – 36 at the time. The doctors had recently given her six months to live due to an aggressive brain tumour. It was a terribly hard time for her and her family. I can't even imagine it. Jalpa and her husband had three young children and were very poor. Her husband earned only a few rupees from daily labour. But I would go and visit her in her tiny room and pray with her, and as we prayed, it was as if *my* spirit was renewed. Jalpa had such a clear vision of Jesus. She poured out her prayers from her love of Jesus, and I could tell that she was somehow seeing the glory of heaven. It was a sacred time for me.

In a similar way, I have also met many people here in Australia who have been told they have a limited time to live. Many of them have shared their faith journeys with me, including **Gwen**.

'I have been healthy all my life ... so it was a big shock to be told that I have leukaemia. It came just two months after my husband, Bob, died of a rare cancer back in 2016. Since then, I've had several trips to the hospital for chemotherapy, and I was in remission for 18 months. But now I'm having chemo tablets and injections, and my doctor says that I have nine months to live, at the most. So, I have written out my eulogy and I've chosen all the hymns. I have the list of Bible readings. Bob didn't write out a list. He stayed well until the last few months. And in the last week, we set up a hospital bed in the living room, and I slept nearby on the sofa bed, and all the kids came and helped. We were all there at the end. He died one night at 9 pm, after we'd been married for 50 years.

But I remember at the end, I asked Bob what he wanted in his funeral service, and he didn't want to talk about it. He probably thought that I would work it out. But I'm different from him. I've planned my whole service. You never know how much time you have left.

In 2016, I had a routine blood test. My doctor rang me afterwards to see if I was all right. "I'm fine," I said. Then she told me that my white cell count was down, and that I needed to have another blood test. So, I had another blood test, and then she sent me to a haematologist, who did more tests.

After those tests, I was at the supermarket, helping with a food collection drive (with our local church), and I walked home. When I got home, I noticed a police wagon waiting outside our house. Two police officers got out and they walked across the

10. Faithfulness to the end

garden towards me, and they said, "You need to go straight to the hospital."

It was a bit of a shock. I think my doctor had been trying to contact me, but she couldn't find me, so she sent the police around. Maybe she was worried that I'd collapsed on the floor. I was in a bit of a tizz, so I rang a friend who took me down to the hospital. They said that I had leukaemia, and it proved to be incurable.

On the whole, I haven't been too sick. But they now say there's nothing more they can do. The thing is … Bob's already there (in heaven) and I'm happy to join him. I'm really looking forward to heaven. I became a Christian in my late teens, and I've always been involved in the church. I can't imagine what heaven will be like, exactly, but I often think about it. I know that I won't have to have any more chemo injections!

So, I've planned my funeral service and I've written it all out in my blue book. At the moment, I'm hoping that my funeral will be after the lockdown (due to the pandemic). I want as many people there as possible, singing! And I'd like them to read John 14:1–7: "Do not let your hearts be troubled. You believe in God, believe also in me. My Father's house has many rooms … And if I go and prepare a place for you, I will come back and take you to be with me …" Jesus is going to come back and take us to be with him. Won't that be wonderful?'

It's a lovely reminder, isn't it? Jesus is preparing a place for us, a home forever. He's getting all of the rooms ready. Gwen is absolutely sure of her eternal home with Jesus. I loved visiting Gwen at her Blue

Mountains home in late 2020 and hearing her story. Her assurance in Jesus was just beautiful to behold. She even showed me her blue book that contained all of her wishes for her funeral, including the Bible readings and hymns. She particularly loved the passage from John 14, and I agreed with her. It's such lovely imagery. Jesus is preparing a home for us with great care.

Since moving to our new home in the Central West, I often think about this passage. We have three guest rooms in our new home, and they're often full, due to visiting family members and friends. That means that I'm often washing sheets, making beds and preparing the rooms with towels. I think about what kind of pillows they want, if the room is clean and if there's anything else that might help them feel more comfortable. That's what Jesus is doing for us! In ways we can't imagine, Jesus is preparing the details in eternity. He is drawing more and more people back to himself, where we will truly belong. He wants to fill up his house! May those truths fill us with great joy today.

There is also an amazing postscript to Gwen's story. Three years later, as I write this, Gwen is still alive! The medical team have found a new drug, and it appears to be working well for now. The drug and regular blood transfusions are keeping Gwen healthy. Praise God for his gift of extra days to Gwen. But the interesting thing to me is Gwen's attitude. Even with that gift of extra days, she still has that beautiful, sharp focus. She still has her eyes on Jesus and her hope in heaven. May it be the same for us, with or without a recent diagnosis.

§

I'm going to finish this chapter with a story from **Tom**. I met him a year ago at the local nursing home not far from our new home. Tom has been living in the nursing home for six years now, and he is not well. He is hard of hearing, and he speaks very slowly and softly. He can't walk at all. To hear his story, I had to lean in very close and concentrate. He certainly said to me, repeatedly, that he would rather be in heaven. But he knows the most important thing, and he kept telling it to me, over and over again: 'I have to hang on to Jesus.'

> 'I started with nothing. I was the eldest of five, and my father was a boilermaker in the shipyards in Glasgow, Scotland. We didn't have hot water, and we didn't have much food. My grandmother was a strongly religious woman, though, and we always went to Sunday school as children. Then we migrated to Australia in 1929, in the middle of the Depression, when I was seven.
>
> Right now, I'm going through the worst period in my life. I'm living in a nursing home. I can't see. I can't hear very well. I can't read. I can't walk. Sometimes I wonder why I'm still alive. I ask God why he doesn't take me. In January next year, I'll be 100. Sometimes, it wears me down. I don't want to die, but I do want to die.
>
> I think about my wife all the time. Her name was Hazel. She was a wonderful woman. The years of our marriage were the happiest years of my life. We started with nothing in Revesby, Sydney. It was all market gardens back then. I was a boilermaker like my father. Then Hazel and I had three children – two girls and one son. We sent them to Sunday school, but I didn't go myself. I never went to church back then. And I didn't go to the war because I was busy building ships, which was very important work. After the war, I went back to tech to

study. I had to sit exams, and I passed them all. Hazel never complained when I was studying. Afterwards, I became the chief welding inspector for New South Wales. If they were going to build a boat (or anything else out of steel), I had to go and inspect it. I ended up travelling all over the state. And we were able to buy a house in Revesby.

Then Hazel died. It was 50 years ago now that she died, but I think about her all the time, every day. She was a wonderful woman. After she died, my two daughters helped me. One of them stayed with me for eight weeks. And my son also helped me. He took me to church. It was the first time I went back to church since I was a boy.

Now my son has died too, and I've been in this nursing home in Oberon for five years. Sometimes, it feels dark in my mind. Last night was like that. I had a dark night, and the darkness felt worse than physical pain.

But in the morning, when I woke up, I thought, 'I have to hang on to Jesus'. That's what the pastor from the Anglican church says to me. He visits me every Friday, and he's the best thing in my life at the moment. He reads the Bible to me, and he talks with me. It really helps me. I know that he's right. I have to hang on to Jesus. I've been better since he's been coming to talk with me. I often wonder why God allows suffering, and I worry about my two daughters. But I believe in Jesus. I believe in heaven, and I pray every night to Jesus. I know that God listens to me. I know that he hears me when I pray.'

10. Faithfulness to the end

It's a profound testimony. Tom is really struggling. He doesn't know why he's still alive, and he wishes he wasn't. He can't hear very well, walk or read anymore. He's nearing the end, and it often feels very dark to him. We might be able to imagine the pain of that kind of darkness. But Tom also knows the most important thing, and he tells it to himself (and his visitors!) every day: he has to hang on to Jesus. And he does that. The local pastor comes regularly to pray with him, which makes all the difference.

It's a needed reminder for each of us. We don't know how it will be at the end of our lives. Will we be able to walk, talk or think? Will we go quickly or slowly? Will we be in pain, or will it feel like sleep? We don't know, but we can pray like Tom. We can pray that we will hang on to Jesus to the end – to his words of hope and healing, to his promise of forgiveness and peace and to the life-changing nature of his presence with us.

One of my favourite verses in the Bible is Philippians 1:6. Paul was writing to the Philippians to thank them for their generous financial gift to him and for their partnership in the gospel. He had been deeply encouraged by them, even while in prison, so he wrote to them about confidence. He said he was sure that 'he who began a good work in you will carry it on to completion until the day of Christ Jesus.' Paul was confident that it was God who had begun the good work in the believers in Philippi, in drawing them to himself in Christ, and he knew it would be God who would finish it. God would hold them close until the last day.

It's a great encouragement to me. God has drawn each of us to himself in Christ. For each of us, our stories are vastly different, but it is God's work through his Spirit that has drawn us into his family. And

God will carry it on to completion until the day of Christ Jesus – until we go to him, or until he returns in glory and makes all things new. It's not our effort or cleverness or hard work. It's God's Spirit at work in us. And that is the greatest comfort, especially on the days or nights when we feel weighed down by the heaviness of this world. Like Tom, we can hang on to Jesus. And we know that we will be held by him.

Epilogue

We've come to the end of our journey around Australia, meeting all of these wonderful people and hearing their stories of faith. I hope you have enjoyed it as much as I have. I hope the stories have stirred your heart to look to Jesus in new ways. I hope they have encouraged you to cling on to God's promises through every stage of your life. I hope they have inspired you to keep pouring out the gifts that God has given you, and to love your communities and the people in front of you, in the places where God has allowed you to be.

I hope, more than anything, that this book has granted you a new, wonderful sense that God is alive and well. He is always drawing us to himself in Christ, all the time, in every moment, everywhere. He is not sleeping, not on hold, not weary and not giving up. He is always inviting and pursuing, transforming and moulding, drawing us to himself every day, invisibly and powerfully, over a lifetime. Indeed, even right now, as we close this book together, God is bringing the right friend, the right words, the right passage of Scripture, the right truth or the right song into someone's life ... exactly when it's needed, even in the midst of the worst kinds of unravelling, perhaps especially then.

For me, as I've been interviewing and writing, I have noticed changes in myself. I have become far more expectant that God is at work in the lives of people around me. I feel like I've been given a fresh lens, and I now find myself regularly in awe of the work of the

Holy Spirit in individual lives. I notice it more. I pause and wonder more at God's goodness and invisible hand in everything. I seem to have an increased expectancy that God will be at work today and every day in the lives of my loved ones. In turn, that has brought new, fresh life to my prayers, which has been deeply needed! I now find myself listening to friends or acquaintances tell me their early, tentative stories about their questions surrounding Jesus, and I immediately imagine the way God will grow those small questions and stories into glorious fruitfulness over the coming decades.

As I write this final section, it is early in 2024 and the wind has picked up around our home. Outside my front window, I can see the wind sweeping across the paddocks, invisible and powerful, catching the long grass and the branches of the pine trees to my left. Immediately in front of me, the dahlias, roses and cornflowers have begun to dance in the wind, and to my right, the boughs of the old apple tree are bending low. Even the purple thistles in the far paddock are not immune to the power of the wind. They are moving in response. The wind is beautiful and wild, unmistakable and glorious, both gentle and full of force, bringing life and transformation beyond my viewpoint.

Perhaps that's what this book is about. In reading the amazing variety of faith stories, we too can see and hear the powerful effect of God's Spirit on our human hearts, unmistakable and glorious, gentle and full of force, wild and beautiful, bringing life and growth and transformation, and pointing us to Jesus, even beyond our viewpoint. We can sit here and marvel at it.

We can be assured that every moment, everywhere, God is at work in lives and homes and families and streets, in Australia and around the world, longing to direct our attention back to Jesus, and longing for us to know him more and more.

I pray that these faith stories and truths will continue to stir our hearts in the years to come. I pray that we will remember, more than anything, that each of our tiny stories is a small part of God's grand story – the story that he has been writing since the beginning of time, and the story that he will bring together in all its fullness when Jesus returns in glory and redeems all things. To him be the glory and the praise, forever.

> *'Oh, the depth of the riches of the wisdom and knowledge of God!*
> *How unsearchable his judgements,*
> *and his paths beyond tracing out!*
> *Who has known the mind of the Lord?*
> *Or who has been his counsellor?*
> *Who has ever given to God,*
> *that God should repay them?*
> *For from him and through him and for him are all things.*
> *To him be the glory forever! Amen.'*
>
> *(Rom 11:33–36)*

About the author

Naomi Reed is a much-loved Australian Christian author. She began writing in 2005 during her family's seventh monsoon in Nepal. Amidst rain, civil war and homeschooling, she discovered a deep love for words and stories, which nourished her soul long after the rain stopped and the family returned to Australia.

Now, Naomi and her husband, Darren, are on the open road with their pop-up van bouncing along behind them, sharing Faith Stories at smaller rural churches and collecting new, surprising stories along the way.

To contact Naomi, go to www.naomireed.info. You can also find her on Facebook at My Seventh Monsoon or Faith Stories/Bible Society.

Other books by Naomi Reed:

My Seventh Monsoon
No Ordinary View
Heading Home
Over My Shoulder
The Promise
The Plum Tree in the Desert
Finding Faith
The Zookeeper
The Conductor
A Time to Hope
Walking Him Home